PRAISE FOR THE 1ST EDITION

"Susan Knox's Financial Basics *is essential reading for any student attending college. Along with a good hug, parents should give this book to their sons or daughters when they begin college. It does not matter whether it is a residential experience or they are living at home and commuting. Every college student will benefit. In addition to providing practical and valuable advice, presented in a very readable format,* Financial Basics *is a seatbelt against financial problems."*

—Myles Brand-President, NCAA,
former President Indiana University
and University of Oregon

"Students have a great deal to manage in their lives away from home—from their coursework to relationships to personal decisions—one of which is how to manage their finances. This book provides credible examples to head off problems and engages both students and their families in pre-emptive planning not only for college but also for life.

A must for parents and students."

—Karen A. Holbrook, President,
The Ohio State University

*"*Financial Basics *has the potential to make an enormous difference in the lives of college students. Research shows that financial problems present some of the biggest obstacles students face in achieving academic success, or even being able to stay in school. Ms. Knox has written a very helpful and accessible guide; it should be required reading for everyone heading off to college. Or for that matter, for anyone who's finding that money problems are tripping them up in their efforts to live effective lives."*

—Martha Garland, Dean of Accademic Affairs,
The Ohio State University

"*Financial Basics: A Money-Management Guide for Students by Susan Knox is an engaging and insightful primer aimed to help young people learn to manage their finances. This book will give practical advice to help the reader avoid many of the common problems encountered by young people who, for the first time in their lives, are responsible for managing their income and expenses. Financial education is sorely missing in our culture. Many parents have poor money management skills. I think that* Financial Basics *should be a standard part of a college's new student orientation program. Financial difficulties is a significant cause of students dropping out of college. Susan Knox's book will help colleges retain students by providing the basic tools needed to effectively manage one's finances.*"

—Jim White, Director,
Student Financial Services, Seattle University

"*Susan has put in this book both the practical and the emotional elements related to credit card debt. Her style and incredible insight give an immediate 'This is me and why didn't someone tell me this before?' reaction from her readers. We intend to use Susan's book as part of our counselor training.*"

—Cuba Craig, President and CEO,
American Financial Solutions

"*After graduating from college I watched my credit card debt grow each month as I learned to deal with a new set of responsibilities. I felt out of control, with no idea how to manage money. I read many books on the subject. Susan Knox's guide is the only one that really made sense to me. The stories are engaging. The tips are easy to understand and achievable. Her book gave me the tools I needed to feel powerful about my finances. Now, two years later I am debt free and building a solid future thanks to* Financial Basics.*"

— Julie Stonefelt,
Evergreen State College, class of 2001

"Financial Basics *is a must-read for every college-bound student who wishes to avoid the disastrous pitfalls that have claimed so many. By sharing the stories of real students, Susan Knox has gone well beyond describing financial hazards. She has arrived at real solutions."*

—K. J. (Gus) Kravas, Ph.D.,
Vice Provost for Student Relations, University of Washington

"Whoever said a CPA can't write for a general audience, especially a young one? They're wrong. Susan Knox has hit a home run. The personal stories draw the reader in. We can all relate to every mistake we, our kids, our students, or friends ever made. Each chapter and paragraph is relevant and important. I especially like the way Chapter 13 ties it all together. Doing what Knox suggests can be a life-changing event."

—David A. Lieberman, Senior Vice President
for Business & Finance, University of Miami

"This book is a must-have for all incoming freshmen or for anyone who wants to finally learn the true basics of personal finance. By sharing her story and stories of others, Susan Knox has made the journey in successful money management real and understandable."

—Anne H. Chasser, Commissioner,
United States Patent and Trademark Office

"The summer before my senior year at Ohio State, Susan Knox asked me to review her manuscript on financial planning for college students. The book contained so much valuable information, in addition to helpful hints, money management, credit and saving strategies . . . it was exactly what I needed to learn about being a smart personal financial manager. My only regret was that I didn't have all this important information when I started college! I would have made much better financial decisions during my four years at Ohio State."

—Katie Chasser Coakley,
The Ohio State University, class of 2003

FINANCIAL BASICS

FINANCIAL BASICS

*A Money-Management Guide
for Students*

2nd Edition

SUSAN KNOX

THE OHIO STATE UNIVERSITY PRESS | *Columbus*

Library of Congress Cataloging-in-Publication Data
Names: Knox, Susan, author.
Title: Financial basics : a money-management guide for students / Susan Knox.
Description: Second edition. | Columbus : The Ohio State University Press, [2016] |
    Includes index.
Identifiers: LCCN 2016004797 | ISBN 9780814253069 (pbk. ; alk. paper) | ISBN
    0814253067 (pbk. ; alk. paper)
Subjects: LCSH: College students—United States—Finance, Personal.
Classification: LCC LB2343.32 .K66 2016 | DDC 332.024—dc23
LC record available at https://lccn.loc.gov/2016004797

Cover design by Lisa Force
Type set in Adobe Palatino

♾ The paper used in this publication meets the minimum requirements of the American
National Standard for Information Sciences—Permanence of Paper for Printed Library
Materials. ANSI Z39.48–1992.

9 8 7 6 5 4 3 2 1

Contents

BEFORE, DURING, AND AFTER COLLEGE

Acknowledgments

First and foremost I want to express my gratitude to The Ohio State University Press under the new leadership of Director Tony Sanfilippo for commissioning a second edition of *Financial Basics* in both print and electronic versions. I also want to thank Laurie Avery for her marketing efforts on the first edition and her support in going forward with this edition.

Thanks to the following people for generously giving their time and expertise to this project: Jim White, Kay Lewis, Robert Haverkamp, Sue Blanshan, Alex Johnston, Wen Lin, Michael Gartrell Jr., Usha Kumar, Frances Foody, Todd Ihrig, Trish Howe, Irene Myers, Mitch Singer, Bill Dillon, T. J. Hatfield, Anne DePue, Sheila Edwards Lange, V'Ella Warren, Kristian Wiles, Raul Anaya, Sue Camber, Kim Durand, Roy Liro, and Mark Westerfield.

My heartfelt appreciation to my community of writers: Priscilla Long, my classmates in Priscilla's writing classes, Andrea Lewis, Waverly Fitzgerald, Shoshana Levenberg, Laurel Richardson, and the Sunday Ink writers.

Special thanks to writer, friend, and first reader Susan Little.

And to my husband, Weldon Ihrig, I express my love and gratefulness for his wise advice and unfailing support. This book is dedicated to him.

Introduction

When *Financial Basics* was first published in 2004, the hot topic was credit cards and how easily students were able to get them and how much expensive debt they were accumulating. That changed with the CARD Act of 2009. Financial institutions were no longer permitted to market credit cards on campus, and certain restrictions made it more difficult for those under 21 to acquire credit cards. Since the CARD Act, the number of students using credit cards and the outstanding credit card debt has declined.

In 2004 there was also concern about increasing student loan debt. University administrators told me that students knew to the dollar how much they owed on their credit cards but rarely knew how much student loan debt they had.

As I talked with students and administrators while preparing the second edition of *Financial Basics,* I found that nothing has changed—there is still confusion and lack of comprehensive information on student loan debt. This knowledge is critical when you are faced with significant financial decisions and for managing your money well.

There are more sources of financial information than ever before. In this new edition, I've given websites and organizations that will help you understand good money-management practices. I've taken the information I've garnered from students and administrators and consolidated them into stories told in a student's voice about lessons learned regarding personal finances. I follow each story with options for handling certain issues and resources for more information.

Financial Basics is arranged in the order you will encounter financial questions—starting in high school as you prepare to go to college, followed by the issues that will come up while in college, and finally, advice about finances when you start your career. You can read this book cover to cover, or you can select a chapter appropriate to your current concerns.

In this second edition, I've added a chapter for parents. Some of the financial issues around funding a college education are specialized, not something parents would normally encounter, and I wanted to bring them to parents' attention as well as encourage them to take an active part in enhancing your financial knowledge. I've also included a chapter for grandparents. Sometimes a grandparent can aid a grandchild in pursuit of a college degree with monetary assistance or other types of help.

My goal in writing *Financial Basics* is to help you, the student, operate from a position of self-knowledge and control to reduce the unknown and anxiety-provoking aspects of money management, and to provide a solid financial basis on which to build the rest of your life in a secure and fulfilling way. My wish for you is that this knowledge will put you on the path to making *smart* financial decisions and to becoming the *master* of your financial life.

Preparing to Go to College

1

My First Checking Account

DRAKE'S STORY

I had a savings account by the time I was five. Every birthday and holiday, cash gifts were divvied up so that half went into savings and the rest was divided between charitable giving and spending money. My parents took me to the bank where a teller would count out the money and deposit it into my savings account. I liked watching the balance grow with my deposits and seeing the interest my money earned.

But it wasn't until I was sixteen that I really got interested in money. That's when my dad took me to his bank and we sat down with a banker. She explained what a checking account is and how I could use it. I learned that my checking account was like carrying cash in my wallet, but instead of pulling out money to pay for something, I could pull out my debit card, and in some instances, I might write a check. And the bank had services that I could use, like transferring funds between my checking and savings account online using my computer or my smartphone. I could check my available cash with my smartphone too. I was cautioned not to overdraw the account—the bank charges a fee for overdrafts and sometimes a merchant will too.

I opened a checking account that day with a $100 deposit, and I received some blank checks, a receipt for my deposit, and a temporary debit card with which I could buy burgers and books and coffee drinks. The official debit card arrived in the mail five days later. I'd already entered my four-digit personal identification number (PIN) at the bank when we set up the account, so I was all set to go.

I couldn't wait to use it. First chance I got, I went to Starbucks and ordered a latte. I swiped my card, entered my PIN on the device beside the register, and I was good to go. I checked my balance with my smartphone app for the bank, and there it was—my purchase at Starbucks for $3.75 and a new balance in checking of $96.25. I was pretty excited with this technology.

My parents wanted me to get used to handling a checking account before I went away to college, so they started depositing my allowance in my checking account every week. When I got a summer job at the neighborhood bakery, I got paid once a week with a check. At first, I walked to the bank, filled out a deposit slip, endorsed the check by signing my name on the reverse side of the left-hand side of the check, and handed both things to a teller at the bank. The teller ran it through a little machine and produced a receipt showing the amount of the deposit and the balance in my checking. Later I realized I could use a bank app with my smartphone to deposit the check. It was easy and efficient. All I had to do was endorse the check, take a picture of each side of the check with my phone, and transmit using the bank app. Sweet.

Dad told me not to endorse any checks payable to me until I was ready to deposit it. He said an endorsed check is the same as cash, and if I lost it, someone could cash it and I'd be out the money.

I'd been warned not to overdraw my account, meaning don't buy things for more money than I had in my checking. I mistakenly did this at Target when I was buying a new Thermos for a hiking date. I swiped my card at the checkout counter, and the cashier said I didn't have enough money to make the purchase. I hadn't checked my balance. I thought I knew how much money was in there, but there was a charge I'd forgotten. While it was an embarrassing moment, I learned to be more on top of my money.

After that I checked my balance before every purchase. But then I got a text from my bank telling me I was overdrawn. I was confused, so I stopped by the bank to talk to the banker who'd help me set up the account.

She explained that a debit card can be used like a credit card in certain instances. Ordinarily when a debit card is swiped in a device that connects electronically with my bank, the purchase and subsequent reduction in my bank account shows up almost instantly. That's the way debit cards work. If I use the card in a situation where I don't enter my PIN but instead sign my name to a receipt, the transaction is like a credit card and doesn't show up until the merchant processes it. That might happen at the end of the business day or it might be a day or two later. So checking my balance when one of my charges had not yet appeared in my account meant I had to allow for enough money to cover it when the charge did come through.

I was embarrassed about overdrawing my account, but she said not to worry—everyone makes slip-ups when they're first starting out. "I know I did," she said. "The main thing is to understand how your account works, what options you have, and keep on top of your activity." Then she told me I could get a text alert when my balance dropped below a certain level. I liked that idea, so I set it at $50. She also said I could get a text every time a transaction went through. I really liked that idea. I thought if something didn't show up right away, I'd keep an eye out for it. I'd mentally deduct that purchase from my balance.

I thought my dad would be pleased with my initiative, and he was, but he couldn't understand why I didn't write down every transaction in the check register I received at the bank when we opened the account. He said he always kept track that way and went online once a week to make sure everything had cleared the bank. If it hadn't, he made a note of it and made sure his bank balance was high enough to cover outstanding charges. I told him I was doing the same thing, just keeping it in my mind instead of going to the trouble of writing it down. He agreed this approach would probably work for me now, when I didn't have that many transactions, but to keep the concept in mind when my financial life got more complicated. I told him I'd take it under advisement. Dad smiled and gave me a look that said, "We'll see."

OPEN A CHECKING ACCOUNT

If possible, get some experience with a checking account before you leave home. Your finances will be simple with a few sources of income and few regular bills to pay, so it's a good time to start.

Many banks offer free checking accounts to students. Opening one will familiarize you with banking and how to manage your money. In some states, if you're under eighteen, you'll need a parent's signature to open a checking account.

Like Drake, you'll probably receive a debit card and blank checks. Some banks will offer a book of checks printed with your name. Chances are you won't need personalized checks, and they will probably cost money. Take the blank checks provided by the bank when you open your account and put them in a safe place. If you find you're regularly writing checks, you can always order personal checks.

PROTECT YOUR CARD AND PIN

You'll be asked to create a four-digit number personal identification number (PIN) that will be used when you make debit card purchases. Don't write this number on your debit card or carry it in your wallet with your card. If you lose the card with the PIN, anyone could access your account. Memorize the PIN. Keep a copy at home with the checks your bank gave you and any other banking documents and information.

Don't loan your debit card or give out your PIN to a friend.

When entering your PIN on a device at the store, protect detection of your number by shielding the device with your body. There have been problems with thieves accessing the debit card electronically and observing the PIN entered on the numeric pad.

MONITOR YOUR ACCOUNT

Your debit card purchases using a PIN are instantly deducted from your balance in checking. You'll be asked by the cashier if you want a receipt for your purchase. Most people refuse a receipt, but there's value in taking one. You can confirm you were properly charged, and you can hold onto the receipt until you make sure it's been correctly deducted from checking. It's one way of monitoring outstanding charges and more effective than Drake's method of trying to keep them in his mind.

Check your banking activity daily to be sure there are no surprises. Look at each individual entry for validity.

One high school student I know spent $4.25 with her bank debit card at a bakery after checking her available balance. She had $5.00 in her account, enough to cover the cost, but the bakery made a mistake and ran the charge twice. She got a notice from the bank that she had overdrawn her account and would be charged $35. She called the bakery. They found their mistake, issued a credit to her account, and gave her four free croissants. She learned of the problem because of the overdraft. If she'd had more money in her account, she wouldn't have known about the double charge unless she'd been regularly reviewing her account.

Remember that credits or refunds issued to your account may take up to three days to appear.

EXPLORE BANKING OPTIONS

Take the time to explore what your bank has to offer. Read through the material you received when signing up for an account. Go online to their website to get additional information. If you have a smartphone, seek out apps that will help you keep on top of your financial information. Drake discovered some interesting options that he made use of: receiving a text warning when the balance reached a predetermined amount, receiving a text notification when a purchase was made and deducted from checking, being able to monitor activity and balances at any time, and depositing checks electronically.

Another option is the ease of transferring funds between accounts. This can aid in building your savings. Either have the bank automatically transfer a certain amount from checking to savings monthly or weekly, say when you receive funds like an allowance or paycheck, or transfer the money yourself.

LEAVING HOME

When you leave home for college, your financial activity will increase with income from grants, loans, scholarships, part-time jobs, and funds from your parents. Your outgo will be more active with payments for tuition, room and board, books, club dues, supplies, and sundries. You may decide to open a checking account at a bank near your campus. But for now, learn the bare bones about managing a checking account so you will be ready to take on more complicated financial management.

KEY TAKEAWAYS

- Open a checking account while in high school.
- Safeguard your debit card, PIN, and blank checks.
- Investigate available bank apps to use with your smartphone. Alternatively, explore your account's online options using your computer or tablet.
- Save your receipts until you confirm the charge has cleared your account.
- Monitor your account.

2

First in the Family

JAMES'S STORY

How did I get to college? It was touch and go. There was no real encouragement from home. My parents hadn't gone to college, and I don't think it occurred to them that I'd be interested. I thought I'd follow my dad's path and work at the garage or learn to be a carpenter. That would have been a fine career for me, but I'm crazy about the work I do now as a mechanical engineer. Yes, I got an engineering degree, but I had a lot of help along the way.

Some of my high-school teachers started talking to me about my future. They were surprised I didn't have any plans for further education. I think they assumed a good student would go on. When they realized I hadn't given it much thought, and when I explained I couldn't afford to go, they encouraged me to explore my options for funding school.

My senior counselor took me under her wing the last two years of high school. When I went in for the routine visit in the fall, she asked me about my plans for more education. I told her it would be nice to go to college, but I didn't see how I could manage it. My parents weren't in a position to help me financially, and I knew college was expensive. On top of that, I didn't know what I would study if I did go.

My counselor suggested something I found very unusual. She asked me to dream about what I'd like to do if I could go to college. I think she wanted me to shift my thinking from a narrow outlook to surveying the possibilities. It was a wonderful lesson for me. I learned there are always ways of figuring out how to do something if it's important enough to me. I went back after a month of thinking about the future and told her my dream.

I knew I wanted to do something creative, *and I enjoyed studying math and science. I met a mechanical engineer at my dad's garage, and as he described his work and what some of his associates had accomplished, I knew I could find satisfaction in that field.*

My counselor encouraged me to start scouting out mechanical engineering programs. She had bulletins from various colleges in her office, the school library had some guides to colleges, and I found a lot of information on the Web.

I was still worried about the money angle. *How would I possibly pay for all of this? My counselor gave me some websites to introduce me to the types of available aid, especially federal and state aid for low-income students. I found www.finaid.org very helpful in understanding the various grants I would qualify for, and I began to understand that grants and scholarships were the best sources of funds because they didn't have to be repaid. I learned that the Free Application for Federal Student Aid (FAFSA) was critical for applying for federal and state aid, and I studied the FinAid tutorial as well as the www.khanacademy.org section that explained the process. Both websites provide information at no cost.*

When I found out I'd need financial information from my parents, I sat down with them and told them the kinds of things I'd need, like their federal income tax return, bank statements, any property or investments they owned. (They looked at me like I was crazy.) They didn't have much, and I knew I'd have to pull this together pretty much by myself. I told them we'd have to do this every year I was in college, and when I explained that it would help me get free money for school, they were eager to do what they could to help.

I began to systematically look at the costs of going to school. I learned that each school has a net price calculator that shows how much grant aid students receive at their school. I also checked out https://nces.ed.gov/collegenavigator/. This website allowed me to compare schools on a vari-

ety of factors including aid, cost, net price, graduation rates, etc. I developed a worksheet so I could lay out the costs side by side. Then I looked at sources of funding—scholarships, grants, and of course, student loans. I was very nervous about borrowing money even though I knew it would be difficult to get through school without loans.

I began to ponder going to our community college *for one or two years so that I could live at home and save money. I investigated distance-learning programs, but I was concerned about getting transferable credits and whether the programs were reputable. I was being careful after I heard about a kid in my neighborhood who signed up for a law enforcement degree with a for-profit college and ended up with over $50,000 in student debt and no job.*

While I wanted to go away to college and have the full experience of living on a campus, my concern with money was more important. I opted to go to the community college for two years. I worked part-time. I got introduced to college life and gained more understanding of the finances of higher education. Those two years, I worked hard at my studies so my grades would be stellar. I hoped to receive more grant and scholarship money. I looked for scholarship money from the beginning, and I applied for as many scholarships as I could. I found that there were scholarships for low-income students as well as for good scholars and other, more specialized types of scholarships. It really paid off for me. After two years, my good record enabled me to transfer to the state university to enter their mechanical engineering program.

I held off borrowing student loan money until the middle of my third year. My parents managed to give me a little money, and I lived carefully. I was intent on not borrowing any more than I absolutely had to. The costs at the state university were reasonable, and they had a good curriculum, but it was a five-year program and meant spending more money for an extra year. I landed good summer jobs, but even so, I graduated with close to $15,000 in student loans. I know this amount is lower than a lot of students have, but I was super careful not to borrow a cent more than I absolutely needed.

Having debt made me nervous, but I knew my starting salary would be at a level so I could repay the loans without too much trouble. In fact, I paid them off in two years by continuing to live like a student. Living a frugal life freed up money I'd have spent on a nicer apartment and car. I knew if I increased my standard of living I wouldn't get out of debt for years, and I decided it was more important to get that part of my life under control so I could enjoy a better life later with no debt pressures. I also wanted to be in a position to help out my folks so they could live more comfortably.

It was the right way for me.

LOOK FOR ASSISTANCE

According to a *University Business* article, 30% of college students are the first in their family to pursue a bachelor's degree, and 24% are first-generation and low-income. Often, the parents of these first-generation and/or lower-income students value higher education and offer a lot of moral support, even if they cannot provide knowledgeable help on college selection. Other families don't know how to navigate the financial aid waters to gather the monetary help needed, and they feel intimidated by the forms to fill out and the information requested.

It's up to you, the student, to seek out assistance. Start gathering information. Tell your teachers and counselors that you want to go to college but don't know how to go about it. Ask them about their college selection process. Talk with students in your community who have gone to college and get information from them on their decision process.

Think about what you'd like to study or possible careers that interest you. Find schools that offer the major(s) you're interested in. Then look at other factors. Go online or check your school library or public library for informative books on college and universities. Review published information like undergraduate enrollment, location (how far from home), the physical size of campus, campus setting, costs to attend, clubs and other social organizations. Then develop a list of colleges you'd like to attend, go to their net price calculator (each school has one). Use https://nces.ed.gov/collegenavigator to provide information on college costs to help refine your list. Another source is www.finaid.org. Or look at www.collegecost.ed.gov. If you have a school counselor who works with college-bound students, seek out this person's help about how to make your selections. Choose the colleges you want to apply to.

FAFSA

You and your family will be required to fill out a Free Application for Student Aid (FAFSA) when you make your college applications. For basic information on FAFSA, go to www.khanacademy.org. Note: All Khan Academy content is available for free.

You'll need information on the family finances, like your parents' income tax return, a list of any assets they own, and debts they owe. You may need to take the lead on this. Filling out the FAFSA isn't fun, but it's the first step in getting funding for college. Skip logic is used to present only those questions the student is required to answer based on their situation so low-income families without much money won't have to fill out the entire form. It's particularly important to file this form so that you can qualify for financial aid. When you receive an acceptance from a school, they will send you a report on how much aid you can expect.

Financial Aid

There are three basic types of financial aid:

- Scholarships
- Grants
- Student loans

Grants and scholarships don't have to be repaid. Loans must be repaid along with interest. Repayment generally starts six to nine months after you leave school—with or without a degree.

Scholarships

Start looking for scholarships immediately. Be cautious about paying for a service to find scholarships for you. You can do just as well using your computer to search for scholarships. Check out www.fastweb.com. Don't forget to look for scholarships given by organizations in your local community. Ask guidance counselors if they have a list of all the local scholarships available. If you know where you'll apply to college, contact their financial aid and scholarship offices and ask for help. Most colleges and universities have extensive websites, and you'll find useful information there.

Continue to search out and apply for scholarships throughout your college career. I talked with one financial aid director at a state university who was proud of the lower than average student loan debt for graduating students and pointed to the fact that her school's students had higher than average scholarship awards. Invest some time in this effort. Remember, you don't have to repay scholarship money.

Grants

The major need-based grants are:

- Federal Pell Grants
- Federal Supplementary Education Opportunities Grants (SEOG)

Need-based means these funds are awarded on the basis of how much money you need to go to the school of your choice after taking into consideration your parents' and your resources. While these traditional grants do not cover as much of the cost of tuition as they were originally intended, it is a potential source of funds for you.

Your state may have grants available or your state may have funds combined with the federal government. Ask your counselor about availability in your state.

Work-Study Programs

Your college will probably have a work-study program. Federal money is provided to pay salaries for students to work on campus. The jobs are usually need-based, so talk with the financial aid office about availability.

Loans

This is funding that will have to be repaid, with interest. Take heart—60% of today's students have loans. The challenge is to borrow only enough money to get your degree. Investigate these federal loans first:

- Perkins
- Subsidized Direct Loan (formerly Subsidized Stafford Loan)

These federal loans are need-based, and interest does not start to accrue until you graduate. The federal government absorbs the interest while you're in school.

If you don't qualify or need more money:

- Unsubsidized Direct loans (formerly Unsubsidized Stafford Loans)

The federal government doesn't pay the interest on unsubsidized loans while you're in school. Interest starts accruing immediately and adds to the balance you'll be required to pay back.

Your institution may make loans available. Make inquiries with the financial aid office.

Finally, there are numerous private loan sources. If you go to these alternative loans, shop around for the best terms. Compare fees, interest rates, and repayment terms before deciding.

Try to delay taking out the Unsubsidized Direct or private loans. These will be your most expensive loans since the interest starts ticking right away. The later you take out these types, the less interest will have been added to your debt when you start repaying.

If your parents are willing to borrow, Parent Loan for Undergraduate Students (PLUS) may be available to them. Parents need to be totally aware of the cost and repayment schedule. For example, interest on PLUS starts accruing as the funds are released, and repayment starts sixty days after the last disbursement for that school year. If your parents decide to borrow money for your education, make sure they take into account the money needed for four or five years of college, not just one year. Each year they'll take on a new loan and additional payments.

LOOK FOR OPTIONS

It may be that you cannot raise enough money to go to the college of your choice. Look for options to keep your costs down. James elected to live at home, attend a community college for two years, work, and save money so he could enroll at a public university for his last three years of school.

Community College

If you plan to attend a community college and later move to another school, check the requirements for transfer. Some public institutions are no longer automatically accepting students from community colleges. Budget constraints and highly qualified applicants have tightened acceptance rates for transfer students. Be sure you understand the rules so you can qualify for admission and have all your credits transfer.

Distance Learning Programs

This is a fast changing possibility in higher education, but be careful. Make sure the credits lead to a degree and/or are transferable. Make sure the program is reputable. Check the Department of Education's website or Google for complaints to see if there is any information relating to bad practices such as promoting unnecessary student loans or offering poor academic programs. This especially applies to proprietary or for-profit colleges.

Military

Can you qualify for one of the military academies or for an ROTC scholarship? Some military scholarships provide funds for the entire program plus a monthly stipend for living expenses in return for service in the military after graduation.

Veterans

If you're a military veteran, search your potential college picks to see if they have an office devoted to military personnel returning to college or attending for the first time. These programs will be useful in guiding you to resources that are specially designed for veterans.

Cooperative Programs

Does your academic major have cooperative programs where you can work in your field for one term and then attend classes for two terms? Engineering programs often offer this option. Ask your academic advisor for funding alternatives that pertain to your field.

Work Through School

Your only option may be that you have to go to school part-time and work in order to get your degree. Many people have done that. It is almost always best to get your degree as quickly as possible because you will earn a higher income once you finish school. But if speed is not an option for you, push on. Academic advisors suggest three hours of study for every hour in class for a B average. Use this guideline to calculate how many coursework hours you can successfully handle.

THINK BEYOND FOUR YEARS

There are a number of examples in my family of people who could not get their degree in the traditional four years. One family member worked full-time at a public university and took advantage of their tuition-reimbursement policy for pursuing a degree.

She took two courses every quarter and got her degree in eight years.

I didn't get my undergraduate degree until I was twenty-nine and mother of two children. My graduation pictures show an exhausted young woman. It was hard, but I never regretted the effort I invested in my education.

ADVOCATE FOR YOURSELF

Ask experienced people for help and ask plenty of questions so that you fully understand your options. If you get discouraging advice, listen, take it under advisement, and double-check with other people to be sure it is accurate. If you're given information you don't understand, find another person to explain the details. I tell my clients that if a financial professional, whether an insurance salesperson, financial advisor, or banker, cannot explain their products so the client understands what he or she is buying, then find someone else to deal with. In my experience, people who cannot adequately explain a product or service may not entirely understand what they're talking about. The same advice holds for financial aid officers and other counselors you consult. You deserve full, understandable answers.

Receiving financial aid is taking advantage of a program that aids citizens to become better educated, which results in a benefit to society. Some of the students I talked with said occasionally they were made to feel as though they were using public funds as if they were on welfare. It was a negative experience and terribly unfair. Borrowing student loan funds is not being on charitable assistance—it's not a free handout.

If you come across negative people, remember they are there to serve you. Also know that many college and university administrators are overworked and under pressure. Perhaps gentle persistence on your part will overcome their attitude. If not, look for another person to work with. Having worked in higher education for a number of years, I know how dedicated most of the staff are and how helpful they can be. Search them out.

TAKE RESPONSIBILITY AND PAY ATTENTION TO DEADLINES

Filling out the forms required for applying for financial aid isn't fun, and it does take time, but there's a payoff for you, so put the effort into getting the forms completed and submitted before the deadline. One student I interviewed keeps a list of important deadlines in his organizer and always follows up with the appropriate office about a week after he submits his paperwork to be sure everything is in order. He believes it's important to establish a good relationship with a financial aid counselor. That way, if he needs help or advice, he knows he'll get personal attention. You may prefer to establish a relationship with a helpful person through email.

If your economic situation worsens, for example, a parent loses a job, go back to your financial aid counselor to determine if that makes you eligible for additional aid. Get to know your financial aid counselor, and when they do a particularly good job for you, send them a thank-you note.

LOAN REPAYMENT

James was nervous about having debt, so he lived in a manner that enabled him to repay his student loans in two years. This was a good decision for him, but it doesn't apply to everyone. Read the chapter entitled "What's Next?" for additional financial help, including student loan repayment options as you start your career.

Take heart when looking at your student-loan debt. According to the Economic Policy Institute, Americans with four-year college degrees made 98% more an hour on average than people without a degree. While it is important to borrow no more than you absolutely need, the cost of your education may be the best investment of your life.

KEY TAKEAWAYS

- Make a list of possible academic majors.

- Make a list of colleges of interest that offer these programs.
- Make a list of the following pertinent information for each program you are considering: the graduation rate (how many students who begin a program receive a degree), the average time it takes to get a degree, the average student loan balance at graduation, and statistics on employment after graduation.
- Go to each school's net price calculator to see how much grant aid students receive.
- Use the above information to refine your list to those schools where you plan to apply.
- Go to https://nces.ed.gov/collegenavigator/ to compare costs among your choices.
- Develop a list of potential scholarships to apply for. Go to www.fastweb.com.
- Make a list of the pros and cons of attending community college for either the first two years and transferring, or completing a degree program there.
- Make a list of experienced people with expertise and advice in funding a higher education.
- Contact these experienced people and make an appointment to talk with them.
- Make a list of older students in your community who have gone on to college with initial limited resources. Contact them and ask them to brainstorm with you on ways to come up with the needed money.
- Explore distance-learning programs.
- Develop a calendar of deadlines for college applications, FAFSA submission, and any other important dates.
- Refine your list of potential colleges.
- Begin your application process.

3

Budgeting for College

SOPHIE'S STORY

When I started my college search, Mom and I made a quick estimate of costs and potential financial aid for each school I was interested in. It helped narrow down the schools I ultimately applied to. After I got an acceptance from my top-rated school, Mom suggested we rework the costs to get a more accurate fix on my finances now that we knew the amount of aid I'd be receiving. Mom's an actuary, so she's really into numbers, and so am I. I plan to major in math in college, maybe be a teacher or follow my mom's example and become an actuary. I don't know yet. I just know I love math, so I thought putting together numbers for college would be fun and useful.

Mom helped me develop a budget for college. *We discussed how we'd pay for college. I'd take out a student loan for part of the tuition not covered by financial aid and be responsible for my personal expenses. Mom would pay for my room and board, and books.*

I began developing my budget by consulting the online information at the college where I was enrolling that gave expected costs for a typical student. I talked with a neighbor who went to the same school I planned to attend and asked her about costs on campus.

I purposely made my budget a generous one, *just to be sure I'd have enough money. Mom said I could adjust the plan after I had some experience and was sure of my costs. We set up the accounts on an Excel worksheet.*

It was fun. I developed a detailed listing of expenses and created a spreadsheet so that I could keep track of everything. I had a line for everything from snacks to laundry to haircuts to shampoo. You get the idea. My spreadsheet filled two pages. It never occurred to me that monitoring my spending in such a detailed way would get me down. But it did. Halfway into the semester I was worn out with accounting. My system required me to keep track of every cent I spent, and my extensive categories meant I was spending a lot of time entering data. I finally decided enough of this and abandoned my system.

Unfortunately, I went from one extreme to the other. *I quit tracking my expenses and spent what I wanted. I signed up for a credit card thinking the monthly bill would provide me with information about how I was spending my money.*

I continued to pay my bills on time but ignored how I was spending my money. I didn't even keep a running total of the cash balance in my checking account. I had plenty of money in my account because I'd deposited all my savings into my checking account so I wouldn't have to worry about bouncing checks. I was done with detail.

When I returned home at the end of the semester, Mom said it was time to review my finances. She didn't know I'd quit following the plan we'd set up. I finally told Mom what had happened. She looked surprised and asked me why. When I explained how budget tracking was so exhausting I couldn't face doing it anymore, she nodded her head in understanding.

Mom apologized. *Can you believe it? She said leaving home and taking on responsibility for my own financial life was a big step and she didn't realize I'd get so overwhelmed by the budget process she'd laid out for me. She said I had to find my own way around handling money. I had to look for those special techniques that work best for me.*

She thought my money breakdown came from my math background— that I believed my finances could be translated into strict mathematical laws, and when there were deviations, it threw me. She said we needed to come up with a new plan.

I returned to my budget and studied my spending when I was keeping track and looked at my credit card statements. I saw some patterns. When I dumped my accounting system and started using the credit card, the "little things" almost doubled. I was spending about $125 a week when using cash, but when I went to a credit card and quit tracking my expenditures, I spent closer to $225. Amazing. I had no idea. I was sure I could keep my cash needs to $125 a week if I paid attention.

This is what I decided to do. At Mom's suggestion, I put my money into a savings account at my campus bank. Every Monday I transferred $125 from savings to checking. This was my allotment for the week, for all the day-to-day expenses like snacks, coffee, eating out, movies, and other small items. Every morning I went online to review what was left of my weekly allowance. I thought about the rest of the week and what I'd be doing that would cost money. That way, if I knew something more expensive was coming up on the weekend, I'd be careful during the week by not overindulging on snacks or lattes.

If I had money left over at the end of the week, I kept it in checking and used it in those weeks when I overspent my allotment. It all seemed to even out over the semester.

I created a simpler, less detailed budget and kept track with a free online app called www.mint.com. I was able to download my banking and credit card transactions and review how I was spending my money. It was so easy compared to my previous method, and I loved tracking my spending with this app.

This system was successful, and I was relieved to have a routine that made me feel in control without all the anxiety. Of course, the key to this method was that I'd tracked my expenditures carefully during the first months at college, so I had good information on my spending patterns, and I knew how much cash I typically spent during the week.

Mom and I had a monthly telephone conversation about how I was doing with my money. It was reassuring to have someone to talk to, and knowing I'd review my financial situation every month helped me stay on target.

I thought a lot about my money-handling lessons. For me, budgets are useful to try to get a fix on the total cost of living. But I learned that a *budget doesn't work precisely as I thought it would. Little things pop up from time to time that simply can't be anticipated. A shower gift for a friend, paying for class handouts, computer repairs—you can't predict these things. That's when I understood why a cushion is important.*

Each month I pay my bills, review my checking account, and generally look over how I managed my money for the month. The key here is generally. I got rid of the shaking hands and fear around money when I stopped being manic about each and every detail. I still paid attention. I knew my financial circumstances. I became responsible about money again. I just needed to find the right way for me to manage my situation.

LESSONS

I cannot tell you how many times I've heard middle-aged clients admit that they can't control their spending. More often than not, these clients were high-wage earners who got into the habit of spending freely, without thought. They had huge mortgages, multiple car loans, and staggering credit card debt. They spent every cent they earned and more. They told me they felt out of control, they didn't know how to stop, and they were beginning to wonder if they could ever retire. Some of them described extreme reluctance and being fearful when it came time to pay their bills. One client was so unnerved by her money issues, she took tranquilizers before she came to see me to discuss her finances. It took a great deal of effort to work with these people to help them change their behavior, and some of them never changed. They'd instilled the habit of spending so deeply and for so long, they couldn't break the chains of debt.

My wealthiest middle-aged clients were steady spenders and savers—people who didn't always make a huge salary but had figured out ways to manage their money within their financial resources and personalities. They had little or no debt—certainly no credit card debt. They had savings, investments, and well-funded retirement plans. They enjoyed life. They didn't pinch pennies. They'd started early in their working years to live below their income and saved a portion of every paycheck.

Your college years are the time to establish good money-management practices that you can follow the rest of your life.

SPENDING PLANS

Because *budget* has a negative connotation, use the term *spending plan* to convey a forward-thinking positive attitude about money with a sense of control. The purpose of a spending plan is so that you'll have an idea of what it'll cost to live as you leave home and go to college. If you track your expenditures for a month or two, you'll see if your original plan was reasonable or if you need to make adjustments. And, understanding your finances is the first step to mastering your money.

Purposes of a Spending Plan

- To know how much it will cost to go to college.
- To determine if you have enough money to go to the college of your choice.
- To plan how to get the money you'll need or adjust your college selection.
- To give you pertinent information when making decisions on expenditures beyond basic needs, such as a study abroad program or joining a fraternity or sorority.

Getting Started

Sophie and her mom had a good approach to developing a list of her expenses for college. They consulted online information available from her prospective college that showed the typical expenses for a college student at her school and in her college town. Those estimates are generic and often conservative, so Sophie further pursued information by talking with older college students to get practical knowledge about college expenses.

It's always wise to add a little extra for expenses. It's almost impossible to create a precise spending plan—either while you are in college or when you begin your working life. Some expenses don't become apparent until you're on campus. This doesn't mean spending plans are worthless. It means you create a plan, monitor your activity, and then go back and adjust.

A Step-By-Step Approach to Estimating Expenses

- Gather information about the cost of attending the schools of your choice. Go online to the colleges you're considering. There should be a suggested budget for each institution with their information for prospective students.
- Adjust the college's suggested costs for anything you know will be different; for example, they show $1,000 for traveling home, but you live nearby, and your cost will be minimal.
- Keep track of your spending for a month. This will give you good information on your daily spending pattern. This is a start. You'll probably have to adjust some numbers when you're actually on campus.
- Add a line for contingencies or unexpected expenses.
- Review your calculations with people who have some knowledge of college costs and keeping track of expenses, such as a parent, a counselor, or an older college student.
- Formalize your spending plan by selecting a budget app and entering your numbers. Mint.com is one free resource, but many apps are available. Your bank may offer a program. Mint.com enables you to set up your spending plan, categorizes expenditures, can give you text messages when bills are due or your account balance hits a certain level, and other features.
- Track your spending for the first month of school.
- At the end of the month, look at the results. Adjust the plan for your actual experience.

MONEY-MANAGEMENT OPTIONS

Many students rely on debit cards rather than cash. It's convenient, most businesses honor them, and the charge goes against checking. Most students don't track their spending when they use debit cards. They rely on the bank to keep track and warn them if their balance is getting low. The danger is overspending. Here are some methods to keep your spending under control.

Envelope Method

Some people like to use the "envelope method" for keeping their spending in line. This is an old-fashioned system of putting cash for the week or the month in envelopes designated for a specific purpose such as groceries, entertainment, or gifts. When the money in the envelope is gone, they have to quit spending. While living in a group setting, it is important to keep the cash-filled envelopes locked up and secure. Even though this may be inconvenient, a number of people have had success with the envelope method, especially when operating on a strict spending plan.

Transfer from Savings to Checking

Another way to manage your spending plan is to keep your money in a savings account and transfer a weekly allowance to checking. This is easily done online. Sophie deposited all her money, $9,500, into her checking account, and that allowed her to ignore how much she was spending. If she'd put the money in savings, she'd earn some interest and be reminded to watch her cash balances in her bank accounts as she transferred money from savings to checking on a weekly basis.

Regularly transferring money gave her an opportunity to think about her financial position and whether or not she was on track. She might not have spent $2,000 more than she planned during her first semester if she'd followed this method from the beginning.

PLAN AHEAD

As you go through your college years, remember to consult your spending plan when contemplating new expenses. The director of financial aid at a small private university told me a good story to illustrate this point. He said the university had a few highly desirable apartments on campus. The right of first refusal went to student leaders. One spring, several student leaders eagerly signed up for the following year. It was a prestigious address, but the students forgot their housing cost would increase by $800 a month. The next fall, the students got their bill. Paying $800 more a month would wipe out any extras they enjoyed, and one student couldn't even afford the new apartment. They didn't look ahead and plan for the new cost.

The group visited the financial aid director explaining they lacked funds and needed help. Fortunately, the director was able to give them additional financial aid, but he now makes sure that prospective renters take into account their higher cost of living before they request a more luxurious apartment.

START NOW

Your college years are a good time to identify and examine your financial predispositions, find the best ways for you to manage your money, and instill good money-management practices in your daily life. That way, when you start to earn a regular paycheck, you'll be ready to take on bigger financial issues such as buying a car, saving for a home, supporting a family, and planning for retirement. You'll feel steady and secure in your ability to plan for your financial future. Life will be easier knowing that you're in control of your financial life.

KEY TAKEAWAYS

- While you're still in high school, keep track of your spending for at least a month to give you a realistic picture of your current expenditures. This is a starting point for planning.
- Gather suggested student costs for the colleges you're considering from their online information. Personalize the numbers for your particular situation and create your spending plan.
- Ask a parent, a family member, or an advisor to review your spending plan with you.

- Track your spending for the first month of college, and then review and adjust your plan.
- Make a list of the ways you can monitor your spending in the future. Choose the best method for you.

While in College

4

Facts of a Financial Life

PHOEBE'S STORY

I was stunned when I received a check for most of my financial aid at the beginning of the quarter. I knew grants, scholarships, loans, and work-study would cover my expenses, and I remembered choosing a box on the financial aid form to have a check mailed to me rather than deposited in a bank account, but I never thought about how it would feel. To tell the truth, I felt rich. My parents rarely had extra money, didn't use banks, and always worked with cash on a week-to-week basis, so I was completely clueless when receiving all that money at once.

My roommate warned me *I'd better get the check in the bank before I lost it. I told her I didn't have a bank, that I didn't know how to open a bank account or what to do once I had one. She suggested I call the financial aid office for advice. They sent me a list of all the banks in the campus area. This was helpful, but I still felt uneasy about walking into one of these places.*

I called my academic counselor and told him about my problem.

Zach understood and asked me to stop by his office. He gave me a booklet his bank provided about the basics of banking and explained the purpose of a checking account. I began to understand that the bank provided a secure way to pay bills and safeguard my money. I learned that the

Federal Depository Insurance Corporation (FDIC) insures most banks so even if the bank failed, my money would be safe.

Zach explained that my checking account would be the repository for all incoming payments like the financial aid check I had and later, my work-study pay. The money going out of checking would be payments like my dorm fees, books, dues for any clubs I might join, food, entertainment, etc.

He showed me how to write a check and told me once I got a bank debit card, I probably wouldn't write many checks, but everyone who has a bank account should know how. Zach showed me a check register that I could use to record the money coming in and going out of the account. He explained that once I had my account set up, I could go online to access my bank information to double check everything was as it should be. This made me feel a lot more secure about my money.

Zach also reminded me that my university ID card could be used to pay for laundry, on-campus restaurants, coffee shops, and for public transportation, but I would have to go to the campus office to add money to the card. He said it was like a debit card, but at that point I was on financial information overload, so I held off until I got my bank account set up.

I nervously went to a bank near my dorm. I explained to the banker that I was a complete novice when it came to banking. She was so understanding and helpful that I relaxed and felt like I could ask her any old dumb question. It was such a relief to get that check in the bank and to know if I had any questions, all I had to do was stop by the office and talk to my banker.

I got a debit card from the bank and learned how to withdraw cash from the automatic teller machine (ATM) that was outside the bank building. As time went on, I learned to transfer money between savings and checking. I had my financial aid money and my paychecks automatically deposited to my checking account, but I had to make sure my money would last for the term, so using Zach's suggestion, I put most of the money into savings and transferred it to checking when it was needed. This way, I earned a little interest (another revelation) and it helped me manage my money so it would last throughout the term.

Later, I saw my friends using their smartphones to make payments and check balances. They told me about getting a text alert if their balance went below a certain amount. I just had to tell the bank I wanted alerts and pick the amount that would trigger a notice. I eventually did all this, but I took my time, made sure I understood what I was doing, and experimented with one thing at a time, like paying dorm fees with my smartphone. It was quite a learning experience, but I now feel confident in my banking skills thanks to the helpful people around me.

OPENING A CHECKING ACCOUNT

You probably only need a basic checking account. Here are some things you should know before you sign up for your account. The information will be in literature the bank provides, or you can work through the questions with a banking person who should be willing and able to answer your questions and help you.

- What kinds of fees does the bank charge? Some examples of bank fees are: monthly service fees, overdraft fees, charges for blank checks, per-check charges for writing more than a certain number of checks each month, and fees for returned checks. Many banks now offer free checking accounts to students. Ask if that's available.
- Where are their ATMs (automatic teller machines) located? If you go to an ATM not run by your bank, you may be charged a fee for using it. Try to avoid paying ATM fees by using your bank's machines. Alternatively, some banks will absorb the cost if you use another bank's ATM. Ask if that perk is available.
- What sorts of features does the bank offer online? Some common items are current balances and recent transactions, text alerts if your account balance falls below a certain level that you designate, depositing checks using a smartphone. These features will save you time and give you the ability to stay on top of your finances. They may offer an online budgeting system. Ask if there are any charges associated with using these features.

- Does your bank have a branch in your hometown and in your college town? If not, how will you manage the account when you're not in town? If you do online banking, have your paychecks automatically deposited or use your smartphone for deposits. You may not need a local branch, but don't forget to ask about the locations of ATMs you can use for getting cash without incurring a fee.

- Does the bank offer overdraft protection? If you write a check or use your debit card for more money than you have in your account, will the bank cover the check using a line of credit similar to a credit card? Your parents may have to co-sign for this feature until you're twenty-one. You have to repay the money used to cover an overdraft, but you'll avoid expensive fees for overdrawing your account. You'll be charged interest until the overdraft is paid. Be sure you understand how overdraft protection works, how you'll be notified if you use it, and how to pay any charges made against the overdraft account. If you can't get this feature, one way to safeguard against overdrafts is to keep a minimum amount in checking, say $250, and don't go below this number. Another way is to ask your banker if they have a service that will automatically pull funds from your savings account in the event of an overdraft. Ask if there are fees for this service.

- What kind of text alerts does the bank offer? Some will text if your balance goes below a certain amount that you designate or when a transaction occurs.

- Does the bank offer a debit card? If you accept, you'll probably be asked if you want a vendor to refuse your debit card if the purchase amount exceeds your bank balance. The alternative is to risk overdrawing your account. While being refused a purchase at the cash register is embarrassing, it will protect you from overdraft fees.

- Does the bank offer a credit card? One way to begin building a credit history is with a low-limit credit card that you pay off every month.

FUNDAMENTALS FOR EVERYONE

Most students use their smartphones, tablets, or computers to transact financial business like depositing a check, transferring money between savings and checking, paying most bills, and checking current balances. You may have that rare occasion where you need to write a check, and your bank will give you blank checks after you open your checking account. You may find the following websites helpful:

- http://banking.about.com/video/How-to-Write-a-Check. htm offers instruction on how to write a check and keep a check register.
- http://www.calculatorsoup.com/calculators/financial/ checkbook-balance-calculator.php#howto why and how to balance your checkbook.

Paying attention to your transactions and balances, thinking about the immediate future in terms of upcoming expenses, having a spending plan, and monitoring spending will give you a feeling of command over personal finances. It's comforting and reassuring. I know you're busy with school and other activities and that you may not take the time to regularly balance your bank account in the traditional way. The following is the minimum effort I suggest you take to keep an eye on your finances.

Check Your Bank Account Online

The charges appearing against your account should be scrutinized regularly for accuracy. Try to review it at least once a week. Some students keep their receipts or photograph receipts with their smartphones for debit card purchases and throw them away or delete the photo when the charge appears on their bank statement. If a charge has not appeared (occasionally it will take a day or two), you'll know that amount should be deducted from the available funds in checking. If your paycheck is automatically deposited to your account, make sure it appears on the correct date. Are there any bank charges you weren't aware of? If you don't understand the charges, email or call your bank for an explanation.

Automatic Deductions

If you have monthly automatic payments, like a gym membership, deducted through your checking account, don't forget them. If you maintain a check register, note the payment at the beginning of the month and deduct it from your available balance. If you don't use a check register, find a way to ensure that you have enough funds in checking to cover the payments when they occur. This is a common problem that creates expensive overdraft charges. Certain apps like Mint will alert you when a bill is due to be paid. One banker I talked with suggested running these automatic payments through your credit card. That way, you don't risk an overdraft, plus you may earn reward points.

Plan Ahead

Sit down at the beginning of the month and plan your expenditures. If needed, transfer money from savings to checking for the month. If you're tracking your expenditures and watching your spending, download information to your budget system and review to be sure you're not overspending in some categories.

Security Issues

You need to protect your financial information, especially when living in a dormitory or apartment with people who come and go, or friends of roommates whom you may not know.

- Don't leave confidential information lying around. Buy a lockbox from an office supply store to store your bank statements, debit and credit card numbers, PINs, blank checks, and credit cards. Put the box out of sight. If feasible, keep this information at home.

- Keep a list of your credit cards and debit cards with the account number and the phone number of the financial institution in a safe place. Don't keep this information with the cards. Put it in another location so that if a card is lost or stolen, you can report it immediately. Speedy reporting of a loss to your bank or credit card company is critical to protect yourself from further liability. Another safeguarding option is to make a copy of every card you carry in your wallet—front and back—and store it in a safe place or ask your parents to keep a copy. If your wallet is stolen, you'll know exactly what was in it and where to report the loss. In most cases, credit card companies assume financial responsibility above $50 for the misuse of your credit card—if you report the loss in a timely manner. Most banks cover you above $50 for the misuse of your debit card.

- Use an app like Password Safe, 1Password, or RoboForm Everywhere where all your accounts are listed with unique, strong passwords that can be automatically generated and periodically changed for each entry. It's like a lockbox where all your accounts are contained with their passwords. All you have to do is remember the main password to get into the app on your smartphone or computer.

- Always use your blank checks in numerical sequence. If you notice a missing check number, review your account online or call the bank to find out the amount and to whom the check was written. If you did not write the check, notify your bank. It's the bank's responsibility to honor your signature only on a check, but it's your responsibility to report the stolen check.

- Keep extra blank checks locked up. This is important because you'll rarely write a check, and if your checks went missing because they're in an unlocked desk drawer, they could be stolen and you wouldn't be aware until you looked at your bank statement—another reason to review your account often.

- If you've written a check for something that is defective or for services not received, and you're worried that the check will be cashed, you can stop payment on the check you have written, provided it has not cleared. The bank usually charges a fee for this service.
- If you receive a check made out to you, don't endorse it until you're ready to deposit or cash it. Once endorsed, it's the same as cash.
- Always use a secured or U.S. postal box for outgoing mail.

Scams

Beware of scams. A campus bank manager told me that scams are increasing. Here are a couple of examples.

Students report being at an ATM after hours when a stranger approaches, saying that he's just received his paycheck in the mail but needs cash and doesn't have an ATM card. The stranger asks if he endorses his check over to them, will they get enough money, say $180, from the ATM to cover his check. They agree, give the stranger $180 in cash and deposit his paycheck into their account. A few days later the student gets a notice from the bank that the check was a forgery. The student is out $180 and has little recourse other than reporting the theft to the police.

Another type of scam is initiated via email. Students receive a request from a company asking them to be mystery shoppers and earn a $250 commission in the process. Their job is to report back on the quality of service provided by Western Union. If the student agrees, a check for $2,500 is sent to them. The student is instructed to deposit the check in their account, write a personal check for $2,250 ($2,500 less $250 commission) made payable to *Cash* from their account, go to Western Union with the personal check, and wire the funds to a designated address. A check made payable to *Cash* is the same as cash. The student never hears back from the company. The check the student received and deposited is bogus and the student is out $2,250.

Just remember, if it sounds too good to be true, it probably is.

Timing

A check or debit card transaction may not show up on the bank records the same day as the transaction, so be very careful about accepting the accuracy of the bank's balance because there could be checks or charges in the pipeline that are not yet deducted from the account. If you return an item, it often takes three or more days for the credit to show up in your bank account. Students get into trouble by accessing their bank balance online and using that balance as the amount of available funds. Most banks will not make deposits available until the check clears the banking system, although a direct deposit or transfer from another account should be available immediately.

Lump Sum Payments

Phoebe had another issue to deal with that could pose problems for the novice money-handler. She received enough money to last for the quarter. Most institutions deduct tuition payments from the grants, loans, and scholarship proceeds, and deposit the remaining funds in the student's bank account. Receiving money in a lump sum at the beginning of the term had posed problems for several students I interviewed. Some ran out of money before the term was over.

The best way to manage funds that will be needed over the term is to set up a savings account with your bank and deposit the lump sum there. Then either ask the bank to transfer a certain amount from your savings to your checking on specific dates or transfer the money yourself as needed. You should be able to do this online. This method will reduce spending errors, and you'll earn a small amount of interest on the money in savings.

Insurance

Be sure you're covered by health insurance. If you've been insured by your parents' policy, have them double-check to be sure you will continue to be covered when you leave for college. If you don't have health insurance, sign up for student health insurance with your college or university.

If you're taking expensive equipment such as computers or sound equipment to college, consider taking out an insurance policy to cover the theft or damage of these items. Your parents' home insurance policy may cover these items, but check with their insurance agent. It might be more beneficial and cost effective to have a separate policy.

Contracts

At some point in your college career, you may decide to move into an apartment or house with roommates. There are some basic ground rules to establish before you finalize your relocation.

- Make an agreement with your roommates on how expenses are to be shared. Put it in writing so there will be no misunderstandings later.
- Read the lease. Carefully review:

    1. length of the lease
    2. rent
    3. security deposit
    4. terms for refund
    5. who is responsible for maintenance
    6. any additional fees such as late payment penalties
    7. whether you can sublet

- Never sign a lease or a contract by yourself. You could be held solely responsible for any unpaid bills. Be sure all your roommates sign every agreement, including agreements with utility and telephone companies. Some utility companies allow only one signature on the contract. If that's the case, select the person to sign and either establish a cash kitty to be funded up front by the other renters for the payments or use an app like Venmo or one provided by your bank so that the roommates can transfer money to the payer's bank account via their smartphones.

- Make sure the rent is paid on time. If not, it could adversely affect your credit rating.
- Check into renter's insurance. Renter's insurance pays to replace the contents of your apartment or house if you lose them in a burglary, fire, earthquake, or some other disaster.

Income Taxes

If you receive wages during the year, you'll receive a notice from your employer in January showing the amount earned and any payroll taxes withheld for the prior year. The form is called a W-2 form, and the information is also sent to the U.S. Treasury office. If you receive a W-2, you must file a federal and possibly a state income tax return. It's not difficult. A one-page simplified form usually suffices. It's to your benefit to file early because you'll probably receive a refund. If you don't receive a W-2 form by February 1, contact the employer for a copy.

Loans

Shakespeare wrote, "Neither a borrower, nor a lender be." It's still good advice when thinking of friends and money. If you loan money to a friend, be prepared to lose the friend and the money. This is harsh, but the reality is that a loan changes the composition of the friendship. While you may have a good relationship with this person, there's no guarantee the loan will be repaid. In reverse, borrowing money may put a strain on a friendship that will ultimately destroy the relationship. And if you're no longer friends, you may feel less compulsion to pay back the money.

Never co-sign a loan for another person unless you're willing and able to take over the payments in the event that the borrower defaults. This situation may arise when someone is borrowing money for a car.

We all want to lend a hand to our friends when they are in difficulty, and I'm not suggesting that you don't help them. Make your decision, ultimately, on whether you can afford to lose money if the other person does not hold up their end of the bargain.

SEEK OUT HELP

Don't be shy about asking for help if you don't have experience in handling money. Academic advisors or university counselors are good sources for directing you to trustworthy information. Bankers are available to give help and assistance. Family members may be knowledgeable. A free online service with short programs about banking and personal finance is www.khanacademy.org, and there are other resources you can Google for the latest information. Learning to manage your finances is part of your education—a critical aspect of living in an ever-evolving monetary world.

KEY TAKEAWAYS

- Deposit large sums of money not needed immediately into a savings account; transfer funds to checking as needed.
- Go to www.fdic.gov/deposit to confirm your bank is a member of the Federal Deposit Insurance Corporation.
- Buy a lockbox to store sensitive information and documents, and keep it out of sight or at home.
- Make a copy, front and back, of credit and debit cards and other sensitive information in your wallet. Store in a safe place and/or give a copy to your parents.
- Set up an automatic alert from your bank to tell you if your account goes below a certain amount.
- Save or photograph debit and credit card receipts until they appear in your account.
- Balance your checking and savings accounts. If short of time, read through all recent charges to ensure they are correct.
- Plan for any automatic, monthly charges to your checking account, like a gym membership, by using an app like Mint to alert you, or run the charges through your credit card, if you have one, to avoid overdrafts in checking.
- If you're renting an apartment or house, be sure all your roommates sign the lease. Purchase renter's insurance.

5

Know What You Owe

DEBBIE'S STORY

I got a wake-up call when I started working in the university's collections office. The collections office mails notices to students, receives payments, follows up on delinquent loans, talks with and counsels student debtors, and turns over uncollectible loans to debt-collection agencies.

As I heard stories of students when they came to the office to complain or ask for help, I realized I'd better be careful about my own student-loan situation. This work experience forced me to think about how much debt I was taking on and how I was going to repay it.

I can't tell you how many people *came into the office insisting they didn't have to repay their loans because they didn't get a job in their field. They were angry and upset. These people felt they should have been warned. They wondered why in the world they were ever approved for such high loan amounts when the job market was limited in their field.*

Some graduates were distraught because their monthly loan repayment swallowed such a big portion of their budget. They were unable to qualify for a mortgage because of their high monthly debt payments. They too questioned why they were allowed to take on so much debt.

That's when I began to understand that students get loans based on their financial need while in school, not on their ability to repay after they leave school. No other type of loan is made in this way. An installment loan or a home mortgage is always based on the earning power of the borrower. I think that's why it's confusing to some students and sometimes their parents.

It was disturbing to observe the number of students who didn't understand what they had taken on when they got loans. Some didn't know that interest would be added to their loans. Some students didn't realize they were receiving money that had to be repaid. Then we encountered the occasional students who had trouble finishing the last few terms because they'd borrowed the maximum allowable and didn't have enough money to complete their degree program. After that, I started keeping careful track of all my loans. I didn't want to get caught in a situation where I wouldn't have enough money to finish school.

__The biggest, lasting impression__ for me was what a burden loan payments were on many of the people who came to our office. I realized I'd better look ahead. I needed to figure my earnings potential when I got my degree. My major was social work. I understood that social workers didn't make big salaries, but I didn't know exact salaries. I went online to find starting compensation levels, estimated my take-home pay, and kept a running total on what my required monthly loan payment would be after I left school. I wanted to be sure that my total monthly payment did not exceed 10% of my take-home pay. I wasn't comfortable with anything higher.

By keeping track and monitoring my debt level, I borrowed less money than I ordinarily would have, and five years after getting my degree, I'm very thankful that I limited myself. It means that I can take vacations, save for a house, and contribute fully to my retirement plan. Being knowledgeable also made me more confident in my financial-handling practices. I didn't worry about money as long as I stayed within the parameters I set up for myself.

__When the collections office failed to collect loans,__ the accounts were turned over to debt-collection agencies. Debt-collection agencies work aggressively to collect monies owed the university and government, and they usually get paid one-third of everything they bring in. Professional debt collectors are tough—I wouldn't want to be on the other end of a phone call from one of them. The person who ran our department fiercely *pursued collections, but she had a heart, too. She trained our staff to listen to the debtors — really listen — and try to help students, but the bottom line was to do our best to collect the debt.*

Observing the collection process, I learned when people run into trouble repaying loans, it's in their best interest to immediately contact the lender and discuss the problem. Most lenders seem willing to work with genuine problems. It saves them money they would have spent finding the debtor, and it saves the debtor a lot of nasty mail and phone calls — not to mention the stress of worrying about the situation.

I was surprised at the consequences *of students not repaying debt after they leave school. If a student drops out for six or nine months, most loans will no longer be deferred, and the borrower will have to start repaying the debt. Sometimes former students can't make the monthly payments. If they quit making monthly payments, the loan will be considered in default, and the borrowers will not be able to get a transcript from their school, and they will not be able to reenter or transfer to another school until they clear the previous loans.*

Federal income tax refunds may be confiscated to pay down the debt, and an employer may be required to send a portion of the person's wages to the loan agency. (This is called garnishing wages). Even if the former student declares bankruptcy, the student loan will remain on file and will have to be repaid.

Sometimes student borrowers would move to a new place or a new town and neglect to notify all their creditors. I can't tell you the number of times students thought if they told one university office of their new address, everyone would have access to the change. Information is not always shared. Students must send address changes to all creditors. Even if borrowers don't receive their mail (perhaps it was lost or stolen), they risk being in default on a loan. I also learned that students don't always open their email or snail mail! That is a big mistake. Even if you don't deal with official correspondence, you're still responsible for your loan — it doesn't disappear.

My advice to prospective student borrowers? *Make sure you understand the loan provisions, and keep a running total of how much you have borrowed and what your monthly repayment amount will be. And don't take on any more debt than you have to borrow to get through school.*

KEEPING TRACK

Debbie makes a convincing case for being aware of what you're getting into when you start taking out student loans. This doesn't mean you shouldn't borrow to get an education. It's a good investment, and you should be able to recover your investment by earning a higher salary than if you did not earn a college degree. But there are some cautionary lessons in Debbie's story.

Make a commitment to keep an inventory of all your loans. On the next page is a form for you to use, or check out your university financial aid's website for online forms that you can access to make a similar document. Create a computer file or a notebook to store all your loan information. Put this Student Loan Master List or a copy from the online system in the front of the file and update it every term. All of the worksheets in this chapter are available at www.financialbasics.org.

Student Loan Master List

Completing the Student Loan Master List will provide the pertinent information of every loan in one convenient place. If you need to contact your lenders for any reason, you'll have easy access to your information. Notice that the fifth line concerns interest. Most federally backed student loans do not start adding interest costs to the loan until the student leaves school and the loan repayment is activated. Non-federally backed student loans and unsubsidized direct loans usually start adding interest to the loan amount as soon as the account is established. This increases the debt more quickly than interest-deferred loans. Try not to take out these early interest-accruing loans until absolutely necessary. For example, if you can delay borrowing these types of loans until your senior year, the loan will accumulate less interest before you graduate and start repaying the debt.

Behind the Student Loan Master List in your notebook, keep a running total of the amount of money you have borrowed and the monthly repayment amount. You can go to www.nslds.ed.gov for this information. This one-page Loan Summary includes columns

Student Loan Master List

Loan #1

Loan Type _____   Account Number _____

Loan Amount $ _____   Interest Rate _____ %

Repayment begins _____   Monthly Payments $ _____

Interest starts accruing: ○ Immediately   ○ At repayment

Loan Holder / Servicer _____

Phone Number _____

Loan #2

Loan Type _____   Account Number _____

Loan Amount $ _____   Interest Rate _____ %

Repayment begins _____   Monthly Payments $ _____

Interest starts accruing: ○ Immediately   ○ At repayment

Loan Holder / Servicer _____

Phone Number _____

Loan #3

Loan Type _____   Account Number _____

Loan Amount $ _____   Interest Rate _____ %

Repayment begins _____   Monthly Payments $ _____

Interest starts accruing: ○ Immediately   ○ At repayment

Loan Holder / Servicer _____

Phone Number _____

Loan #4

Loan Type _____   Account Number _____

Loan Amount $ _____   Interest Rate _____ %

Repayment begins _____   Monthly Payments $ _____

Interest starts accruing: ○ Immediately   ○ At repayment

Loan Holder / Servicer _____

Phone Number _____

for keeping the balances of the total amount borrowed and the monthly payments when the loan is activated for repayment.

Loan Summary					
Loan #	Repayment Starts	Amount Borrowed	Total Amount Borrowed	Monthly Payment	Total Monthly Payment
1					
2					
3					
4					
5					
6					
7					
8					
9					
10					
11					

By using the Loan Summary, you'll always know your monthly debt obligation after you leave college. If you set a target amount for monthly payments like Debbie did, you'll easily know when you're getting close to your limit. That knowledge will keep you on top of your financial situation, and you'll feel in charge. For some people, a lack of knowledge creates a nagging worry that saps energy. With the Loan Summary, you won't have that problem.

Here's a positive example of the value of keeping a running total of your loans. In 2012, Indiana University sent a letter to each student with loans giving the total amount borrowed and estimating the final total at graduation along with the monthly payment required. The next academic year, borrowing declined by 12.4%. It's clear that knowledge is power, and students responded to a concise report on their borrowing in a positive way.

Debbie was concerned about repaying her student loans on a social worker's salary. She did a smart thing. She acquired starting salary information for her profession in the towns where she was interested in living. This information is available from the Bureau of Labor Statistics website, www.bls.gov/ooh. Consult a counselor in your college for additional help to develop this salary number.

Debbie took her calculations a step further. She figured out her take-home pay and tried to estimate her costs of living. It's so easy to think of an annual salary and forget to deduct income taxes and other expenses withheld from the paycheck. You can expect at least a 25% to 30% reduction in your pay because of various withholdings. There are federal income tax, usually state income tax, often city tax, and FICA (Social Security). You also may have health insurance, short-term/long-term disability insurance, life insurance, and retirement plan contributions deducted from your paycheck.

To project your take-home pay, use the Monthly Take-Home Pay worksheet. Notice that there are three columns. You may be considering more than one profession. Or, you may be contemplating different places to live. Use the columns to look at your options.

Monthly Take-Home Pay			
	Career/City	Career/City	Career/City
Monthly Salary			
Less Payroll Deductions			
Federal Tax (15%)			
FICA (7.6%)			
State Tax*			
City Tax*			
Medical Insurance			
Retirement Contribution			
Disability			
Other			
TAKE-HOME PAY			

*These vary depending on where you live. Find out the exact amounts, or, if you aren't sure where you'll be living, use estimates of 4% and 1% respectively to estimate state and city taxes.

PLANNING AHEAD

Debbie had a goal of not exceeding 10% of her take-home pay in student-loan payments. By getting an estimate of her salary expectations and payroll deductions, she took the first step to assure herself that she could meet this financial requirement. Some financial advisors suggest that total monthly debt repayment, including student loans, credit cards, and car loans but not rent or mortgage payments, should not exceed 15% of take-home pay and, if you find yourself approaching 20%, start working to get some loans paid more quickly. In the final analysis, it's up to you to decide how much debt you want to assume.

Another way to assess your appropriate debt level is to estimate your monthly expenses after you leave school. Use the Monthly Living Expenses worksheet I've provided for you. Start by using your current expenses and adjust the costs according to your best information. For example, you know what your student-loan payments will be by using the Loan Summary. Check the classifieds online where you plan to live to get an idea of housing costs. If you plan to buy a car, estimate the monthly payment plus operating expenses. Plug in 10% of your take-home pay in the savings column. When you are finished, add all the expenses, deduct them from your take-home pay, and see what's left.

If you find your take-home pay will not cover your living expenses, you need to rethink your decisions. There are two basic areas to consider—you either have to make more money or reduce spending. Could you make more money and be satisfied with your work if you chose another career? Can you reduce your student loan borrowing to a level that allows you to follow your career decision? This might mean living a more moderate life while you are in school or transferring to a less expensive college.

Sit down with a counselor, a wise friend, or a parent to review your thinking. Sometimes another person can come up with ideas that you've not considered. Or, you and your friends could pool ideas for possible options; for example, public transportation might alleviate the pressures of owning and maintaining a car.

Having this information will allow you to make better decisions as you go through college. You won't wake up in the middle of the night wondering if you'll have financial problems when you start

Monthly Living Expenses			
	Career/City	Career/City	Career/City
Rent			
Utilities			
Food			
Transportation			
Student Loan			
Other Loans			
Clothing/Personal Care			
Recreation, Entertainment, Gifts			
Charitable			
Savings			
TOTAL EXPENSES			
TAKE-HOME PAY			
TAKE-HOME PAY LESS EXPENSES			

working. You'll not suddenly find yourself in the workforce with burdensome unanticipated debt that restricts your ability to enjoy life.

KEY TAKEAWAYS

- Estimate how much you'll have to borrow and the total monthly loan payment to complete your college degree.
- Determine how you'll keep track of your loans throughout your college years.
- Go to www.financialbasics.org for all the worksheets referenced in this chapter.
- Create your ongoing Student Loan Master List and Loan Summary worksheets to keep track of all student loans. Update annually or whenever you take out a new loan.

- Find out when the first repayment of your student loans is due and when interest begins to accrue.
- Research your future career, find out the potential salary, and estimate living expenses and loan payments.
- Use the Monthly Take-Home Pay and Monthly Living Expenses worksheets. Subtract living expenses from your estimated take-home pay to see if you're overextending your debt.
- Notify all lenders when there's a change to your mailing or email address.
- Don't ignore letters and email from your university or lenders.

6

Credit Card Phobia

SLOANE'S STORY

I was in middle school when I heard the stories about my big brother Jason and his credit card problems. He came home one weekend near the end of his first year of college and confessed he'd gotten into deep debt and asked for Dad's help.

At that time, credit card companies were able to set up tables on campus for students to sign up for a credit card, no questions asked. Jason also got credit card offers in the mail every week. By the end of his freshman year, Jason had five credit cards in his wallet, all maxed out, and he couldn't make the monthly payments. Jason had over $5,000 in high-interest debt. My parents were shocked.

Jason talked to me about his troubles *because he didn't want me to have the same problems. He said he spent a lot more money when he used a credit card. Paying for his purchases was delayed, and it didn't seem like real money, so he kept spending.*

Jason said getting the cards made him feel proud that a bank trusted him, and he thought if he made the minimum payment each month, he was being responsible. He didn't realize how much interest was being tacked on to his balance every month, and it seemed like the minimum payment didn't do much to reduce his balance.

Jason gave me an example. "If I bought a $20 pizza and financed it through my credit card at 20% interest, at the end of the first year, that pizza would be $24 (20% of $20, or $4 interest plus $20). At the end of the second year, the cost would be $28.80 (20% of $24, or $4.80 interest plus $24). I saw that I was paying interest not only on the pizza, but also on the previously charged interest. Making the monthly minimum payment only made a small reduction in debt because of the interest. But the credit card companies don't figure interest once a year; they add it every month or even daily so that the debt is growing even faster."

Jason said that to get out of this mountain of debt he had to get a part-time job and really pare his spending to the bone. In addition to working, he had to keep his grades up to maintain his scholarship. He reached his goal of paying off his credit card debt before he graduated from college and before he had to start paying back his student loan debt. He felt good about that but regretted the things he couldn't do like attend a concert or go to a fancy restaurant with friends once in a while because he'd been so careless about money his first year of college.

I vowed in middle school never to let that happen to me. I now know that there's a law that prevents credit card companies from coming on campus and setting up tables at football games or on the quad with free t-shirts for signing up for a card the way they did when Jason was in college. I'm thankful I don't have to resist the enticement of easy credit, but to tell you the truth, after my brother's troubles, I don't think anything would have persuaded me to get a credit card. They're dangerous. That's the message I got.

I went on a strictly cash basis—debit cards, bank app for payments and deposits, cash, and an occasional check. I was not taking any chances. I paid my bills on time. I looked at my bank transactions every morning and matched up the charges on my debit card with the receipts. I never went below $100 in checking, but just to be safe, I also got a text alert from my bank when my balance hit $125.

My life was in order. I was proud of my money management. Then, my junior year, I decided to rent a house with four other students. The landlord checked our credit history to see if we'd be reliable tenants and pay our rent on time. Three of us didn't have any credit history. The landlord refused to rent to us. Fortunately, our parents backed us up by co-signing the lease so we could get this great house near campus. I loved living there.

The landlord was a nice guy, and he took the three of us aside and advised us to look at ways to strengthen our credit history. "Look," he said, "When you get out of college and start interviewing for a job, buying a car, and renting your own apartment, you're going to need a credit history. Employers often check with one of the three big credit bureaus—it's one way to assess your responsibility. Car companies check before they'll sell you a car on credit, and, as you know, landlords check too. I've heard that professional schools like medicine and law check before admitting students. They don't want their students dropping out of the program for financial reason."

This was news to me and my friends, so we asked around about how to establish a credit history and get a good credit rating. That's when I heard the dreaded words—get a credit card. I couldn't believe it. I asked the manager at my campus bank, and that's what he told me. Actually he told me a lot more.

"You can't get a credit card until you're twenty-one, but if your parents sign for you or if you have a part-time job or other sources of income, we can issue a credit card in your name," he said.

"But they're dangerous," I said. "People get into debt using credit cards."

"That's true, and that's the challenge for you. Get a card with a fairly low credit limit, say $400. Charge about $120 every billing cycle and pay off the balance every month. This will show that you've received credit and are responsible by not using more than one-third of your credit line and by promptly paying what you owe every month. If you can do that, you'll be on your way to establishing a credit history."

"But I have student loans. Doesn't that count?"

"Are you making a payment on them every month?" the banker asked.

"No, they don't have to be paid until I graduate."

"Right. That's why you don't have a credit history. You're not making regular payments yet. I'll bet your cell phone plan is attached to your parents' plan and you don't make monthly payments for that either. Once you graduate and start paying on your student loans, and taking on other monthly obligations, your payment activity will be reported to the credit bureaus."

I reluctantly signed up for a credit card. My parents were happy to co-sign for me because they knew I wouldn't abuse the credit. Even so, they warned me not to skip a payment because it might reflect badly on their credit history since their names were on the account. Whew! How complicated can finances get? I thought I had it all figured out and was playing it safe, but I guess there's a middle ground when it comes to having a credit card.

PROS AND CONS OF CREDIT CARDS

When I first wrote *Financial Basics,* I would have applauded Sloane's reluctance to get a credit card because there was such widespread abuse. Students were collecting credit cards right and left and racking up expensive debt. I was a lot more concerned then with students' lack of understanding of how to properly use credit cards than I was about establishing a credit history.

But now I see there's a middle ground between the temptations of credit and having one credit card to build a good credit history. Your college years are the perfect time to test how credit cards will affect your spending patterns. It's an opportunity to understand your financial profile.

For example, are you a spender or a saver? Do you feel euphoric after a shopping trip only to feel guilty the next morning as you survey your purchases? You're probably a spender, so you need to determine the best ways to control your impulses.

If you're a saver, you'll be less inclined to binge-spend, but caution is still advised. Most people find they're less careful with their money when using a credit card rather than cash. It doesn't seem like real money. The bill won't come due for a month, and they feel like the money will be there, somehow.

Let's look at the pros and cons of having a credit card.

Credit Card Cons

- Losing control. When using a credit card, you can lose sight that you are spending your own money and overspend.

- Damaging your credit score. If you max out the card every month or are late on payments or don't make the minimum required payment, your credit history and your credit score will be adversely affected.
- High-interest rates. If you don't pay off the balance every month, you'll be charged interest on the unpaid balance, making that pizza you charged a lot more expensive. Minimum monthly payments are usually based on a ten-year repayment schedule, and interest is charged on interest, month after month. This is the way compound interest works against you.
- Rewards chasing. If you get a credit card for rewards like airline miles, cash back, or points, you may be tempted to spend more to accumulate the rewards.
- Wrecking your spending plan. With a credit card, you may forget all about your spending plan and not notice how much you're spending in any given month.

These are cautions, real dangers to having a credit card, but the advantages are persuasive too.

Credit Card Pros

- Useful in emergencies.
- Easier to rent a car.
- Easier to dispute a charge. You can ask the credit card company to put a hold on the payment of a questionable charge. The business whose charge you dispute will be more attentive since they haven't been paid.
- Protection. If your card is lost or stolen, most credit card companies will assume financial responsibility after the first $50 of illegally charged purchases. Your job is to immediately notify the company of the loss.
- If you have an automatic monthly payment charged against your checking account, say a cell phone bill, it's safer to run the payment through your credit card than through checking because if you forget the charge is coming up, you may inadvertently overdraw checking, incurring bank charges.

- To provide security. Debit cards are more vulnerable to electronic theft and since they're tied to your checking account, your cash in checking is vulnerable if you are negligent with your card.
- To provide a concise record of spending that can be easily downloaded to your computer so you can monitor where your money is going.
- To build a good credit history.

PROCEED WITH CAUTION

I am still cautious about recommending a credit card for students because I've seen too many adults fall into deep expensive debt because they were addicted to spending. Having credit cards exacerbated their obsession. They couldn't stop spending, and it scared them.

Even careful shoppers tend to spend more when using a credit card rather than cash. But this is a good time for you to test the waters with a low credit limit, observe your spending habits, see if you can be responsible, and find techniques for good credit card management.

SELECTING A CREDIT CARD

If you decide to get a credit card, use caution when selecting the financial institution. While the CARD act of 2009 eliminated aggressive on-campus recruitment of students by credit card companies, some companies are soliciting students through the mail, and I don't like what I'm seeing. Let me give you an example.

A client's college-bound high school senior received a personalized credit card application from an out-of-state financial institution. The envelope included a note for parents reassuring them that their child could have their own credit card without the parents signing for it, and it was a good thing. They said much of the same things I said about the pros of a credit card. Looking at the application, the company was able to get around the CARD Act by asking the student to check off any sources of funds or income like summer jobs, scholarships, work study programs, savings, grants. Then they were asked how much they expected to receive from these sources each year. This qualified the student under the CARD act as having income sufficient to pay their own bill.

I looked at the interest rates on the application. The card had a 0% introductory annual percentage rate (APR) for one year. After that, the APR was 29.9%. That's extremely high interest, even for a credit card. I went online to see if there were any complaints about this company. There were plenty.

This company starts out offering a low credit limit—$100 or $200. After the person starts using the card, the company begins raising the credit limit into the thousands. Many credit card users succumb to the temptation of higher limits by making more purchases and running a big balance, just as Sloane's brother did.

A calculation of simple interest on an account balance of $1,000 owed with a 30% interest rate would add $300 to the account after one year. But these companies don't add interest once a year; they add it daily on the unpaid balance so that with a customer making the minimum monthly payment, the interest will add up to more than $300 a year. There were other complaints of aggressive collection calls, difficulty in reaching the company by phone, rude employees when they did connect, and broken promises of forgiving late payment fees.

If you decide to sign up for a credit card, ask the bank where you have your savings and checking accounts if they will issue you a credit card. Or use the company your parents or a trusted friend recommend based on their experience. If you receive an offer in the mail, it's best to shred the application rather than take a chance on a company's business practices. One company uses a symbol and colors of a well-known credit card company, but their practices are similar to the example cited above.

CREDIT CARD MANAGEMENT

If you get a card, give yourself some guidelines for using it.

- Pay off the card every month, and if one month you cannot pay in full, don't use the card until you can pay the debt.

And if you can't pay in full one month, always, always pay at least the minimum and be sure to pay it on time.

- Start off with a low line of credit, one that if you can't manage your spending and max out the card, you'll be able to pay it off in a few months.

- Keep your charges at one-third of your credit limit; for example, if you have a $600 credit line, charge no more than $200 per month ($600 divided by 3). Later on, when you apply for other loans, like a car, your credit score will be higher. A good credit score means the interest charged on the loan will be lower.

- If you find you can't control your spending, either cut up the card or ask your parents to hold it for you. When you feel ready to try again, ask for a replacement card or retrieve the one held with your parents.

OTHER CREDIT CARD MANAGEMENT TECHNIQUES

- Study your behavior using a credit card versus using cash. Does your decision making change when you use the card? Are you having difficulty viewing the card charges as real money? Do you buy things with your credit card that you wouldn't buy if you were operating on a cash basis? What could you do to change? Maybe it's a red dot you stick on your card, and when you see that dot, it's time to stop, reflect on what you're buying, and decide if you can afford it. Maybe you put the card in a hidden place in your wallet so it's not so easy to pull it out and you have time to think about what you're buying and whether you need and can afford the purchase.

- Consider giving yourself a weekly charging limit. Examine your credit card balance online every morning. If you approach your weekly limit, stop spending until the following week. This is similar to my earlier advice of getting cash every week for incidentals or transferring a certain amount from savings to checking every week and stopping when you run out of money. You'll gain a feeling of control, and the knowledge of your credit card balance will ease your worries about overcharging.

- Sometimes a credit card company will generously offer to increase your line of credit. You don't have to accept their offer. If you're satisfied with your limit, write or call the company and tell them you don't want your credit line increased. Later, if you need a higher limit, you can request an increase.
- If you get home after a shopping trip or an online spending spree and realize that you've spent beyond your means, return your purchases.
- Have the store hold an item you're interested in purchasing for twenty-four hours. This will give you time to coolly reassess your ability to pay and whether you really want or need the item.
- Go online at least once a week to review account charges to ensure there are no mistakes or erroneous charges and that any credits to the account are made (credit for returns, etc. sometimes take up to a week to appear on the statement).

KEY TAKEAWAYS

- When getting your first credit card, request a low credit limit until you know that you can manage the card.
- Do not carry charges of more than one-third of the card's limit in any billing cycle.
- Pay off the full balance every month.
- If you overspend in one month or don't have the funds, be sure to pay at least the minimum payment and don't use the card again until it's paid in full.
- Never skip a credit card payment.
- Always pay before the stated deadline to avoid extra charges.
- Consider giving yourself a weekly charge limit.
- Go online at least once a week and review charges to your account.

7

Spend, Spend, Spend

LESLEY'S STORY

I'm an accountant, so I should be an expert on financial management, but if potential CPAs were screened for their ability to handle money, I'd never have been accepted as an accounting major. I've been a disaster with money. I never thought about repaying the loans I took out. I never analyzed whether or not I really needed the money. I got as much money as I could, and I spent it. Now, twelve years later, I'm still paying off my debts.

The first lesson I learned *was not to try keeping up with my peers. I had a group of friends who had more money available to them than I did. I thought I had to keep up with them to be accepted. It never occurred to me that we could be friends without me spending money the way they did.*

I joined a sorority—an expense that wasn't in my budget. I made some wonderful friends, but they had a lot more money than I did. We ate out often, which meant I was paying for meals at the sorority house as well as at restaurants. We loved movies and often went to concerts and clubs, which took another chunk of money I hadn't planned on spending. Then I needed a different wardrobe so I would fit in. It was a huge expense. I learned how to shop for nice things from my sorority sisters and how to live the good life, but I ignored my financial reality.

My solution was to apply for student loans. I also applied for credit cards and department store charge cards. I could've gotten a job during the school year to cover some of these additional expenses, but I was afraid it would cut into my social time. And to be perfectly honest, I thought my friends would look down on me if I worked.

I hadn't planned to take a trip during my freshman spring break, but all my friends were flying to Mexico, and I desperately wanted to go with them. That's when I discovered university emergency funds. I found out I could borrow up to $1,800 for sixty days, and I made a bee-line for the office. Mexico was beautiful. I never thought about how I would come up with the $1,800 in two months. I had to beg the administrator to renew the loan for me until I could get the money.

By the end of the school year, I knew I had to make extra money during the summer to pay off some of my debts. I found a second job and thought I'd use those earnings to pay back the emergency loan and erase my credit card debt. It didn't work out. By fall, I'd hardly made any progress on my bills, so I signed up for more student loans. I didn't give it a single thought—I filled out the paperwork and looked forward to fun times with my sorority sisters.

Later on, I realized I tend to want things now and plan to pay for them sometime in the future—I tell myself I will somehow earn or receive money to cover my purchases. It's like knowing you're getting a cash gift for your birthday and spending it over and over again before the money arrives.

Since I was always short of cash, I charged the entire meal when we went out to eat, and my sorority sisters gave me cash or transferred money to my checking account via their smartphones for their portion of the bill. I used my credit cards at the ATMs to get cash. I didn't realize that a higher interest rate was charged against a cash advance—it was over 22% interest. I probably paid more in interest than I originally charged on my credit cards.

I continued to apply for and receive student loans. I never thought ahead about repaying the loans, never considered what that would mean in monthly budgeting or even if I would be able to pay it back. I had this idea that the university was protecting me. I thought they wouldn't give me the loan money if I couldn't repay. I didn't understand my obligation to take responsibility for my debt decisions.

It's hard to believe that I could have been so naïve and simple-minded *about these things. But it happened, and twelve years later, I'm still living with the consequences.*

My out-of-control spending went on for two years *until I decided to get married. I had a beautiful wedding with my sorority sisters in attendance. I decided to drop out of school and work until Brian finished his degree. It never occurred to me my student loans would come due six months after I left school. Talk about denial. What an upheaval that caused at home when I started getting the bills.*

After some big arguments, Brian and I sat down and listed every debt, the interest rate, and the monthly payment. It was staggering. I had $25,000 of debt in student loans and credit cards. I was earning barely enough to make ends meet and send Brian to school. There simply wasn't enough money to cover the monthly student loan and the credit card payments.

We felt completely stymied—we didn't know what to do. Finally, I talked it over with my parents to see if they could help us.

They were stunned by the amount of debt I had. They had no idea I could get that much money without their knowledge. They told me to go to my financial-aid counselor at the university and ask for advice. They also suggested I cut up all my credit cards.

I couldn't cut them up. I needed the financial security the cards gave me. Brian convinced me to get rid of all but one credit card, and he put it in a safe place. At least I knew I had it; it just wasn't as accessible. I started using a debit card that deducts automatically from the checking account. I still had tremendous urges to spend money, but I noticed that using the equivalent of cash made a difference in how I felt about buying things. I evaluated purchases more carefully knowing the money would come right out of checking.

Fortunately, my parents kept us afloat until we could figure out what to do. My financial-aid counselor warned me that if I ever wanted to get back in school again or transfer, I'd have to be careful to make regular payments on my student loans. I didn't realize that if I got behind on my payments, the university could deny me admission and withhold my transcript if I tried to transfer to another college.

Brian and I talked about declaring bankruptcy. *I thought it might be the best way to stabilize our situation—the stress on our marriage was incredible. I learned bankruptcy wouldn't erase the student loans. I'd still* *be responsible for paying them. After much discussion, Brian and I decided we had a moral obligation to repay all our debts.*

I went to the Consumer Credit Counseling Service office for assistance, and they helped me work out a reasonable repayment schedule on the credit cards and told me how to contact creditors to negotiate monthly payments we could manage. My parents reluctantly agreed to handle the student-loan payments until I could pay them. I got a second job, and Brian worked as well.

Our financial burdens overwhelmed our marriage. We were only twenty and unequipped emotionally to handle it. We sought a counselor at the university for help in our marriage, but when I got pregnant a year later, the relationship became more and more strained. We finally separated when Shelby was six months old.

It's been tough, but I'm getting back on my feet financially and emotionally. I managed to get a college degree this year by working and going to school part-time. If I'm careful for the next ten years, I'll be free of debt by the time I'm forty. Now that I have a better-paying job, I pay with cash, and I'm careful not to add any more debt. I only borrow money for my car, and one day I hope to buy a house.

I've not had an easy life since I got into debt, *and I worry that Shelby won't have all the things I'd like to give him. He'll be going to college around the time I finally get out of debt, and believe me, I'll be sure he understands how to manage his money before he leaves home.*

A PENCHANT FOR SPENDING

There is a lot to learn from Lesley's story. The first lesson is that a student has to get comfortable with her financial status and grounded in herself as a person. Lesley is not the first person who spent money she did not have in order to impress others. But what a price she paid. She is now thirty and still paying for things she bought as a student. And, she doesn't have any prospect of relief for another ten years.

I've seen people fall into this spending mode like they are sliding down a slippery bank into a pond. No matter what they do, they can't seem to climb out of the water. The reason they can't get out is because they can't stop spending. They complain about their lack of discipline, they worry a lot about their debt, they even envision themselves on the street when they are old and unable to work, but they don't stop spending.

If you have this penchant for spending, now, while you're young and relatively debt-free, is the time to conquer this inclination. You'll know if you have a problem by the way you spent your money while in high school. If you find that you spent all your money, even though you knew you needed to save for college, that is one sign. If you have a feeling of excitement when you spend only to be followed by feelings of remorse, that is another indicator. If your friends remark on all the things you have compared to them, maybe you should take a look at your collection of possessions.

CONQUER SPENDING COMPULSIONS

How can you come to grips with your spending compulsions? Study how and when your spending gets out of control. Are there certain conditions that lead to excesses? Perhaps you are bored or worried and shopping relieves that feeling. Instead of buying an item, ask the salesclerk to hold it for twenty-four hours. This will give you time to cool off and reconsider your decision. If you bought the item and now believe it was a mistake, return it to the store. Find another activity to relieve boredom or worry. Maybe a walk would help or meditation or a chat with a friend.

Keep the credit limits on your credit card low until you know you can control your spending. If you can't control use of your credit card, cut it up. Use cash or a debit card instead. Look for other ways to curb your spending. Ask your parents and friends what they do.

Make an appointment with a counselor at the student health center. Professional counselors can help you explore the reasons for your spending and can assist you in finding ways to change your behavior. Consider the Consumer Credit Counseling Service as a resource. There are also organizations that can help, such as Spenders Anonymous and Debtors Anonymous.

FUTURE MONEY

The second lesson: understand the mind games Lesley played on herself. She always thought she could pay for her purchases in the future by getting another job or using birthday money. She admits she spent future money more than once, and her debt kept mounting. This compulsion to spend can be addictive, and Lesley was hooked. Remember her reluctance to cut up her credit cards. She couldn't do it. She had to have one card available just in case the urge to spend returned.

It's so easy to talk yourself into spending future money. For example, if you have a tax refund coming for $1,000, it usually takes about six weeks from the time the tax return is mailed to the Internal Revenue Service until the check arrives in the mail, three weeks if you file online and have the refund automatically deposited in your checking account. Six or even three weeks can feel like a lifetime, and it's easy to get excited about a $1,000 windfall. You start dreaming about spending the refund now to bring immediate satisfaction into your life.

You feel entitled to something special, so you buy a new spring wardrobe using a credit card or cash that is needed later in the school year. You know the refund check is coming, and you plan to replace the money at that time. A few weeks later, the check arrives. With the heady prospect of having extra money in hand, you spend the refund a second time.

If you have the inclination to spend future real or imagined funds, acknowledge this tendency and promise you won't spend the money until you have it in hand. Think of this not as denying yourself, but protecting yourself.

It can be difficult to resist spending, but if you can devise a plan to manage your money and follow the strategy for a few months, you'll detect a change in your behavior. You'll notice a feeling of being in control instead of wildly rushing off to spend anticipated funds. You'll lose those feelings of remorse. You'll feel grounded around money and steadier in managing your financial life.

KNOW THE RULES

Lesley's third lesson was to monitor her student loans and understand the rules of repayment. She dropped out of school without a thought to the fact that the loans would have to start being repaid if she were not attending classes. She learned that not making the monthly payment could affect her ability to return to school later on. And she discovered there was no escape from the loans—she couldn't declare bankruptcy to get rid of them. Her only option was to negotiate a lower payment that she could meet or go back to school so that the loans would be deferred until she graduated from college and got a better-paying job. That's a lot of pressure for anyone to endure.

Lesley had no idea how much she owed or what her monthly payment would be. I recently talked with a student-loan officer who said that students consistently underestimate the total loan money they have borrowed. Even though students may have thousands of dollars of debt in student loans, the number they know, almost to the penny, is how much available credit is on their credit cards. I believe the reason for this is that student loans are deferred for payment and there is no monthly statement reminding the borrower. Credit cards are in the present, and payments are required each month, so students see how much credit is still available.

KEEPING TRACK

There are several reasons for keeping track of your student loans. First of all, there's a limit to the total debt you can borrow against governmental sources. I recently heard a story about a fourth-year medical student who had maxed out her loan money by the end of her third year. She had no idea how she was going to finish her program, and she had close to $200,000 in debt to repay. If you keep a running total of your loans, you can be sure not to exceed the limit. Look at the worksheets provided in this book. Ask your financial-aid officer what the borrowing limit is for your baccalaureate degree. Write that number in red ink at the top of the Loan

Summary worksheet or highlight it on your computer spreadsheet so that you will always be aware of your limit.

Review your loan status before the new academic year starts. Could you manage with less student loan money than the year before? The less you borrow, the less you will have to repay. And if you find at midyear you underestimated your financial need, many loans permit additional funding during the year to make up a shortfall.

It's a good idea to keep the monthly payment you will be required to make on your student loans in your mind as you approach graduation and job hunting. Use the simple forms provided in this book and you will always know your total debt and the monthly payments. This knowledge will help you decide how much more you're willing to assume in debt each year and how much you can afford. You'll be able to compare monthly take-home pay in your chosen profession to the amount of monthly debt repayment you are assuming.

Remember this useful rule of thumb: your total monthly debt payments, including student loans, car loans, and other personal loans, should never exceed 10% to 15% of your take-home pay.

VISUALIZE THE FUTURE

If you can keep your borrowing to a minimum while in college, you'll have a lot more money when you reach the work world and want to buy a car and furniture, contribute to a retirement plan, and save for a home and a secure future. By limiting your debt, you'll have more freedom to pursue your dreams and you'll have options. You won't be stuck in a job you discover you don't like but cannot leave because you have too many financial restrictions. That's what debt is—a restriction on your life.

Getting a college education is a good investment, even if you have to borrow money to achieve it. But be careful not to take on frivolous debt. Don't fund a new wardrobe with student-loan money. You'll be paying for it years after you get your college degree.

KEY TAKEAWAYS

- Take a look at how you spent your money over the last month. Write down the purchases that were extras—wants, not needs. How did you pay for these purchases? Where did the money come from? How do you feel about those purchases now? Would you buy them again?
- Make a list of all your student loans. How much do you owe?
- Investigate the terms for repaying all your student loans— when repayment must begin and the total amount of monthly payments. Keep a running total.
- Teach yourself how to spend money on important things for yourself, not to spend money to impress others or to make friends.
- Have the courage to say, "I can't afford this," or "It's not in my spending plan this month," or "I'm saving up for the Study Abroad Program next year so I won't be able to go out to dinner tonight." What are other helpful phrases that will help you say no to spending money you don't have?
- Devise ways to help curb your spending. What sorts of aids can you come up with?
- If you are having trouble with spending, seek out a counselor to help you or join an organization such as Spenders Anonymous or Debtors Anonymous.
- Remind yourself that when you manage your spending, you're not denying yourself—you're protecting yourself.

8

Building a Credit History

MADISON'S STORY

I'll be honest. I didn't always pay my bills on time when I was in college. I don't know why. I had the money. I didn't have that many bills to pay—credit card, smartphone, quarterly club dues—but I hated sitting down to do it. I told myself I was busy with school—I'd get to it later. So I let my payments slide for a month or so. I received late notices, but the companies didn't seem too upset. I figured it was no big deal. I was actually saving time by only paying my bills every other month. It turned out to be a big deal, but I didn't discover that until I graduated from college.

I moved to Minneapolis *from Cleveland to start a new job as a business manager with a small college. I hoped to live near the campus and was excited about getting my own apartment.*

I located the perfect place about two miles from campus and arranged to rent the apartment. I didn't realize that the manager would run a credit check. Two days later, she called. She said I had a history of late payments on some of my bills while I was in college and she needed a larger deposit than she originally said. Instead of the first and last months' rent, she required a six-month deposit on my place. If I paid my rent on time for one year, she'd return the extra four months' deposit at the end of the year.

I was in shock. Thanks to a generous graduation present from my godmother, I had a start-up fund to get established in Minneapolis. My godmother pointed out that I'd have a lot of one-time expenses getting my new life in order, like buying a work wardrobe, renting an apartment, making deposits on utilities, and furnishing my new place. A six-month rental deposit would cut my little start-up fund to the bone. I wouldn't be able to furnish my place as I imagined, and I had to scale back my plans for a car and new clothes.

I hated being blindsided *like that, and I made up my mind to find out what I could do about my financial records and determine if I could get my record changed. When I opened my new bank account in Minneapolis, I asked the banker how I could get more information. He explained that there are three organizations, Experian, Equifax, and TransUnion, that collect financial data, and I could request a free copy of my credit report from these firms by going through* www.AnnualCreditReport.com.

I was amazed at the amount of information already collected on me. I'd been late with my credit card payments and my cell phone bills. All of my late-payment history appeared in the report. In addition, I'd written a bad check once (after that I got overdraft protection for my checking account), and the retailer had reported the bounced check to the credit agency. Plus, all my credit cards were listed. One was an account I'd taken out at a department store during a special promotion, and I never used that card again. I even forgot I had it.

I went back to my helpful banker *with the credit report and asked what I could do to get rid of the negative information. I learned it could take up to seven years to clear my credit report. In the meantime, I'd be paying higher interest rates for loans because a bank or another creditor reviewing my report would feel I was less likely to repay a loan and that represented more risk to the lender. He wasn't surprised that my rental deposit had been increased. He said every day a tenant doesn't pay rent costs the landlord money in lost revenue. I was upset, but I pulled myself together and asked him what I should do.*

The banker told me not to add any more credit cards or department store accounts. He said it was tempting to cancel the credit cards I wasn't using and didn't want, but since I was trying to clear my report, a cancel-

lation would be another negative. It usually takes about two years to clear cancellations, and I should wait to cancel the credit cards until a time when I knew I wouldn't be requesting new debt, like a mortgage or new car loan. He said it's like a double-edged sword: cancellations count against the credit score, and having too many credit cards also count against it. When I asked why, he replied that even though I might not have any charges on these cards, the fact that credit was available would count against me when I tried to get a loan. Available credit is the same as having debt as far as a lender is concerned. If I cancelled a card, it might appear the company cancelled it, which can be viewed as a negative. That's why it's best to time canceling credit cards to a quiet financial period when I won't be applying for a loan.

He suggested when I decided to cancel my cards to send a letter by certified mail to the credit card company requesting they cancel my account and to be sure they noted that it was canceled at my request. This would eliminate a canceled credit card showing up in my credit report as though the company had canceled me. A copy of my letter along with the mailing receipt should be placed in my permanent files.

The tough part was clearing my credit report. My banker explained that even though I'd be able to get a loan for the used car I'd found, I'd end up paying a higher rate of interest because of my poor credit history. He reminded me it could take up to seven years to improve my credit rating and advised me to be patient, to pay my bills on time, and always pay at least the minimum amount required on my credit card bills. I was somewhat relieved when he said that some financial institutions looked more carefully at the latest two years of activity rather than the whole history. That made me even more determined to follow his advice.

It's been four years since I graduated from college, and my apartment is furnished the way I hoped it would be, and my car loan is paid. I make sure to pay my bills on time. I'm getting married in a few months, and we plan to buy a house. I hope my credit report will pass a mortgage company's scrutiny.

I wish I'd known how much information was being collected on my financial life while I was still in college. I didn't realize I was building a credit history. I'd have been a lot more careful if I'd known.

CREDIT REPORT VS. CREDIT RATING

Just to be clear, a credit report is a summary of your credit history that contains a listing of your credit cards, student loans, your other debts, and whether or not you pay your bills on time. A credit rating or credit score is a number, often called a FICO score. The originators designed a formula for gathering a person's credit history and translating it into a single number. There are some other companies who also generate credit scores. FICO scores generally range from 300 to 850—the higher the better.

CREDIT REPORTS COUNT

While interviewing a group of students who were willing to talk about their financial practices, I met a student who seemed intent on trying all kinds of ways to manage his money. His latest approach was to pay his bills every three months. He said he was too busy to do it more often. He had no idea his behavior was being recorded and would make life more expensive and difficult later on.

Most students, though, wonder how and when they should begin to build a credit history. They're aware that a good credit history will be important as they begin to look for jobs, buy cars, and apply for mortgages, and that employers are increasingly accessing credit reports on potential employees as another way of assessing the person's background.

While college students have an awareness of the importance of one's credit rating, the knowledge about the process seems to be lacking. One of the comments I hear frequently from bankers and other financial professionals is that college students are ruining their credit ratings by not paying their bills on time.

Why Your Credit Report and Credit Score Are Important

- Employers review credit reports as part of their assessment of a potential employee.
- If you go on to a graduate or professional program like law

or medicine, your credit report may be reviewed, and if you have too much debt, you may be asked to delay starting the program until you've reduced your debt to a manageable level.

- Your credit history will impact the interest rate you'll pay to borrow money, including a car loan and a mortgage. The better your credit score, the lower the interest you will pay.

What Makes Up Your Credit Score

- 35% is paying bills on time.
- 30% is your debt. Note: Maxing out credit cards is detrimental to your score. Keep your credit card debt at no more than one-third of your credit line.
- 15% is your credit age—the length of time you've had a debt accounts. The longer you've held a credit card or some other debt instrument, the more beneficial to your score.
- 10% is account diversity: a mix of credit card, car loan, mortgages, and student loans—a mix is considered stronger information.
- 10% is how much applying for new credit—if you apply for a bunch of credit cards at one time, this will show up as a negative.

Even though you're at the beginning of collecting a financial history, look at how much you can affect your credit score right now. Sixty-five percent of your score is based on paying bills on time and not maxing out your credit cards. The other components will take more time to accrue, but keep them in mind as you get your first job and begin to add more to your financial history. Check out www.creditkarma.com for free credit score information.

Banks Collect Data

In this high-tech age of constant information transfer, much of our financial activity is being recorded in a central data bank. This information is shared among member banking institutions. Writing a bad check or skipping a monthly payment to a bank is very likely to appear in this data bank. Even inadvertently closing a checking account without sufficient funds to cover outstanding checks and charges will show up in your records. This kind of negative information might lead a bank to refuse giving you a new account. Imagine not being able to open a checking account.

Before closing a bank account, note any outstanding items and quit using the account until all charges have cleared the account.

LOOK FOR OPTIONS

If you have difficulty paying your bills on time, look for solutions to enable you to keep your credit rating strong. Many organizations will automatically deduct a payment from your checking account or charge it to your credit card each month. This will ensure that your payment is always on time. The trick is to remember the bill is coming due and to make sure there's enough money in your account to cover the charge. Running the payment through your credit card is a safer option to prevent bank overdrafts.

There are several ways to pay bills online. Some banks offer this service, and some companies will allow you to set up a mechanism or use their app for paying their bill online.

Try paying your bills as soon as you receive your statement. It will seem easier to get the bills paid if you divide the work into smaller segments. Paying your bills as soon as you receive them will make you feel more powerful about your money.

Apps like Quicken or Mint are available to track financial data and import bank data to balance your checking account. They provide reminders for routine payments like rent or telephone bills. Do a search for reviews of the latest apps and software to determine what will work best for you.

BEING OPEN ABOUT MONEY

Madison is getting married in a few months. Should she tell her fiancé about her financial history? Absolutely. This isn't something a partner wants revealed after a few months of marriage and it *will* be exposed when they apply for a mortgage. Undisclosed or unresolved money issues can be devastating to a marriage. Both partners need to share their current and past financial data. Order credit reports and review them together. This is good starting point to establish how to handle money as a couple. If there are disagreements about personal finances, it's wise to consult a counselor or financial professional about money-handling options and come to agreement on how to set up a financial arrangement that's fair to both people.

KEY TAKEAWAYS

- Go to AnnualCreditReport.com or call them at 1-877-322-8228 and request a free copy of your credit report. Review it for accuracy and to gain information about what your report contains.
- Use www.creditkarma.com to find your credit score.
- List all the techniques you can think of to make sure you pay your bills on time.
- Determine your best way to be sure you pay your bills on time.
- Contact your creditors before the payment is due if you can't make a payment.
- Request a copy of your credit history before you graduate from college and start job hunting to ensure there are no erroneous entries.
- When you move, be sure you submit your address change to all lenders and your bank.
- Before closing a bank account, be sure all outstanding charges have appeared on your statement.
- Before you enter a permanent relationship with another person, review your credit reports together and discuss how you'll handle money as a couple.

9

Car Crazy

RON'S STORY

I loved my car. I took good care of it, changed the oil regularly, made sure it was clean and polished. It was a shiny black used Jeep Grand Cherokee, and I loved cruising around campus. I thought I could afford the Jeep, but I badly miscalculated.

My mom tried to talk me out of getting a car before I went to college, but I'd had this dream since I was little, and I wasn't going to let it go. I'd saved enough to buy the car so I wouldn't have a monthly car payment. Mom worried a car would cost too much money while I was in college. But once I owned the car, I figured out a budget for college including the car expenses. It was tight, but I knew all the costs: gas, insurance, and maintenance. My dad said the car was in good shape, so I was certain there wouldn't be too much expense beyond normal maintenance, most of which I planned to do myself. I was convinced I could manage all right.

I was right. It was great having a car. I made a lot of good friends, and I always drove when we went out. Sometimes they would ask me to take them places to run errands or take them home for the weekend, and I was happy to help out. It was cool to have so many friends during my freshman year.

The problem was I was beginning to run short on money. I thought I had everything figured out, but by the end of the first term, I knew I had messed up my calculations. There were costs I'd never thought of when I set up my budget. First of all, I had to pay to park my car on campus, a quarterly fee of $425—a lot of money, and I hadn't put it in my already-tight budget. Sometimes when I was running behind schedule and didn't want to be late for class, I'd park at a meter or in a closer parking lot. I got a lot of tickets. I couldn't believe it. A ticket at an expired meter cost $40, and if I parked in the wrong lot, I found a $60 ticket on my windshield. I tried to pay them, but sometimes I didn't have the money, so I tossed the ticket in a drawer, thinking I'd pay it later.

I'll never forget walking down to the parking lot one Saturday night with my friends. We'd planned a big night. When we got to the lot, I couldn't locate my Jeep. I thought it was stolen, and when I called the campus police, they informed me the car had been impounded because of all my parking tickets. I had to get a ride to the impound lot and pay the tickets, plus towing costs and the impound fee. It came to $750. I had the money, but it wiped me out for the rest of the quarter. When I called home for money, Mom told me they couldn't spare any more and I'd have to figure out something else. At least she didn't say, "I told you so."

A friend told me about the university emergency loan fund, and I borrowed $750, but I had to pay it back by the beginning of the next quarter. I asked for more hours at the bookstore where I worked part-time. Working extra hours took time away from my studies, and my grades slipped. My scholarship contract said I had to maintain a certain grade average to continue to receive money.

I started to get a little nervous about all these problems when I learned I was eligible for a credit card because of my bookstore earnings. This might be the answer. I signed up right away and got a $1,000 line of credit. I felt good—the bank thought I was trustworthy. I had things under control again.

When the beginning of the next quarter rolled around, it was time to pay off the emergency loan. I'd planned to use a cash advance from the credit card to pay the loan, but I didn't have enough availability in my credit line. In fact, I'd charged over $800 on the card, a little more than the cost of getting my car out of hock. I'm not sure where that money went.

I maxed out my credit card by taking a $200 cash advance, but I was still $550 short. I went back to the financial aid office and asked for another loan of $550. They gave it to me, and I used it and the $200 from my credit card advance to pay off the previous quarter's university loan. I was a little uneasy about taking on another loan, but hey, I didn't see what else I could do. My car expenses were a lot higher than I'd planned. I didn't realize how many miles I'd be putting on the car. I spent a lot on gas, changed the oil more often, and when I hit a big pothole, I had to replace one of the tires.

I went home for the summer and landed a job with a manufacturing company in town. It was hot, heavy work, but it paid better than anything else I could find, and I hoped to get some overtime work. I had to make as much money as I could during the summer break.

My mom noticed I was getting credit card bills and asked me what was going on. I explained that I'd figured out how to get the extra money to cover my car problems by using a credit card and the university's emergency loan fund. She was surprised and upset, too. My parents don't have a lot of money, and it worried her that I was getting into debt even before I began a full-time job.

That night my parents and I discussed my debt. I had $1,000 in charges on my credit card. As my mom pointed out, I had spent $1,000 more than I planned for my first year in college. I realized that if I kept going at this rate, I would have $4,000 in debt when I graduated from college. My mom corrected my calculations.

"Look, Ron, when you graduate you will have $4,000 in debt, plus the interest you are being charged on your balances. Making the minimum monthly payment will hardly put a dent in the debt. And when you took a cash advance, they charged you an even higher rate of interest. You're paying 15% interest on your purchases and 22% on that cash advance you took to pay off the university emergency loan. It's like a runaway train of additional costs."

She pointed out that the minimum monthly payment is based on a ten-year repayment schedule, and I would probably pay at least another $4,000 in interest. To be honest, I hadn't even thought about the cost of borrowing money, and this was one fast, painful lesson on the power of compound interest.

Mom addressed another problem. I needed to look at how much money I'd need to live on campus next year and how I'd pay for it. I was earning

$15,000 from my summer job and part-time work, my parents were chipping in another $10,000, and my scholarship was $2,000. So that's $27,000, but it looked like I needed $28,000 a year to cover all my expenses. With a sinking feeling, I knew the answer to my budget problem. I'd have to give up my car.

Then I had an inspiration. My parents and I had tried to make my undergraduate educational funding work without borrowing student-loan money, but now it made more sense to borrow money that I wouldn't have to pay back until I graduated from college. The interest rate would be a lot lower than the credit-card rates, too.

Dad reminded me that I'd planned a strategy of paying for my undergraduate degree so I could continue on to professional school. My original game plan was that I would not borrow any money until I went into dentistry. I knew dentistry would cost a bundle—probably around $70,000 a year, and I'd have to borrow at least $20,000 a year. It seemed smart to keep my costs as low as possible while I was in undergraduate school, because I knew later I was going to take on big debt.

Then my dad really blew me away. He said, "As I see it, the problem is that you want to finance your car twice."

He went on to say that if I borrowed student-loan money, I'd have a $4,000 debt just for operating the car. I wouldn't be debt-free when I graduated from undergraduate school. In fact, I wouldn't finish paying for the Jeep until after I started working as a dentist because the student loan repayments would be deferred until I got my DDS.

Why would I want to borrow money to drive a car I couldn't afford and start paying off that loan six years later when I might not even have the original car? I realized it was better to give up my car now and wait until I had extra income.

I sold the Jeep at a $4,500 loss, but with no car expenses, I was able to cover the loss and pay off the credit-card balance in less than a year.

I missed my car. But I kept telling myself someday I'd have an even finer one. And it was a relief not to be so worried about stretching my money to cover all my expenses.

Now I'm in my last year of dental school, and I'm glad I didn't waste student-loan funds on a car. I borrowed a lot of money to go to dental school, but that's an investment in the work I want to do—an investment that I will recoup by earning a good living and doing work that I enjoy.

EMOTION VERSUS FACT

Emotions play a big role in the way we handle money. Sometimes we want something so much that we subconsciously skew our information gathering so that we can have what we want immediately. Ron's love of cars and his strong desire to have a certain image overtook his innate common sense.

You'll notice that Ron did not figure out his spending plan until after he bought the car. He believed that somehow he would make his money cover the extra costs of owning a car. When he drew up a spending plan, he realized that money would be tight—but he left no room for error in his plan.

Ron had another problem—he didn't know the full costs of owning a car. As he developed estimates of the costs of getting a higher education, he needed to go to multiple sources for complete information. The costs for parking a car on campus are in a list of fees that the university provides. Reading that list carefully for any fees he might incur and talking with other experienced people about the costs of owning a car at college would have reminded him of expenses he hadn't considered.

EMERGENCY FUND

Ron didn't take into account emergencies and unforeseen events. There are two things he could have done to protect himself. First, he needed to add an amount to his spending plan for flexibility. It's very difficult to construct a precise spending plan. You always need to build in a little extra money to cover the unknown. By doing this, you'll make a better informed decision on whether your desired purchase is really possible within your income.

Ron also needed an emergency fund—some money put aside in a savings account that he never touched except in case of an emergency. The blown-out tire qualifies as an emergency. The ongoing parking tickets and subsequent impounded-car costs qualify as emergencies too, but he could've avoided the onslaught of tickets after receiving the first one.

It's hard to have an emergency fund when money is tight, but if at all possible, try to set aside $350 to $1,000 for this purpose, even if you don't have a car. One source of emergency funds might be an income tax refund. Commit to putting your tax refund check aside for emergencies. It will give you a feeling of security and prevent you from using costly cash advances from your credit card or borrowing from other sources.

If you're afraid you'll be tempted to spend the extra money in your emergency fund, put the money in a separate account or in another bank that's not quite as accessible. Alternatively, open another account at your bank that requires two signatures for withdrawals—you and another trustworthy person who will help you decide if your withdrawal truly qualifies as an emergency.

CONSIDER YOUR OPTIONS

Ron could have asked himself the question, "What will happen if I don't have a car on campus?" This was a tough question for Ron to entertain—he really wanted that car. But it's a good question to ask yourself whenever you are considering any purchase that is nonessential and may put stress on your finances.

Ron could've decided to wait a year before he bought a car. Living on a residential campus usually reduces the need for personal transportation. Other modes of transportation might have been adequate. Public transportation may have been sufficient. A bicycle could have been the answer. As far as trips home, the cost of a bus, train, or plane tickets might have been a lot less than the cost of a car over nine months of school.

These options for transportation are not always apparent until one is living in the actual situation. If Ron had waited until the end of his first year, he would've had a lot more knowledge to make a decision.

EVALUATING LOANS

Some students believe that it's okay to take on debt for extras while in college because they will be earning good money when they graduate. If you get into this habit, I can guarantee you will always have debt.

Money borrowed to invest in your education makes sense. You are investing in yourself, and the average college graduate earns significantly more over his or her lifetime than a high school graduate. If you need to borrow money to pay tuition and basic living costs while in college, that's a reasonable investment. Student loans are usually at lower interest rates and often don't start accruing interest until after you graduate.

It's wise to consider the long-term effects regarding your financial decisions. Ask yourself if you want to be paying for your college car years after you've bought a new car (and taken out another loan for the new car). And, if you do, ask yourself if you really want to use student loans or expensive credit cards to fund the car expenses. In many cases, a car purchase is not an allowable use of student loan funds.

WHEN TO SELL

Some students caught in a financial bind say they can't afford to sell their car because they'll take a loss. That's not always true. If the student considered the savings generated by eliminating the car, car payment, insurance, gas, and maintenance, the loss would be recouped over time. If you're struggling to make ends meet, gather the facts and examine the possibilities.

Add up all the money you spend each month on the car. Don't forget to include the monthly cost of insurance and any other additional costs that are paid less frequently, like the license and parking fees.

Find out how much it would cost to pay off the car loan and the current market value of your car. Subtract the car loan from the market value. If you have a gain or break even, selling the car will relieve your finances immediately.

If you have a loss, divide the loss by the monthly costs. The result is the number of months it will take to break even. In Ron's case, he had to cover a $4,500 loss on the sale of the car, but he saved $500 a month in operating expenses. It took nine months ($4,500 divided by $500) for him to break even. Ron borrowed $4,500 from his bank. His father co-signed the loan. After he repaid the loan, Ron had $500 extra a month, which he saved for dental school.

LEASING

Leasing is attractive when on a limited budget because the monthly payments are less. But before you sign a lease, educate yourself on the particulars. The reason lease payments are generally lower than car-loan payments is because you're paying for the use of a car over a certain time frame. The leasing company owns the car and estimates the value at the end of the lease period (usually four years). The lease cost (what you pay) covers the difference between the full price of the car and the residual value of the car at the end of the lease, plus interest.

Before you sign a lease contract, remember that you're committed to making those payments for the full time period. If you decide you can't afford the car midway into the lease, you'll have to arrange with the leasing company to sell the car. You'll probably pay a stiff penalty for breaking the lease, and you'll have to cover any loss associated with the sale. And this assumes that the car can be sold. When the economy slowed down, car lots were full of leased cars waiting to be sold because lessors had lost their jobs and couldn't afford their cars. The lessors had to continue the monthly payments until the car was sold.

Take into account the restriction on the number of miles you can put on the car during the lease period. It's usually ten to fifteen thousand miles a year, and if you exceed that restriction, there'll be additional costs to pay when you return the car at the end of the lease.

If you decide to lease, ask what interest rate is used to compute the lease payment. Compare that number to car loan interest. If the lease interest is higher, try to negotiate a lower rate. It doesn't hurt to ask. If the car company says there's no interest, rephrase the question and ask what financial factor was used.

KEY TAKEAWAYS

- Analyze car-ownership costs for gas, licensing, insurance, maintenance, parking, and emergency situations such as parking tickets or new tires.
- Explore other transportation options at your school.

- Wait a year before buying a car.
- Don't finance short-term, nonessential purchases with student loan money.
- Gather facts about selling the item before you make your decision about whether to keep or sell it.

10

I'll Think About It Tomorrow

ALAN'S STORY

I went to college with a generous allowance. My parents paid my tuition and my room and board—everything. Later on, I got my own apartment and had to pay rent, utilities, and other household expenses, but my parents increased my allowance to cover those costs. You'd think I had it made, but I'm a put-it-off kind of guy. I focused entirely on school and my social life. I didn't pay much attention to my finances. I didn't open my bills or online notifications. I said I'd get to them later, but I never found the time.

But not taking care of my money preyed on my mind. *I woke up at night worrying about bills, promising myself that first thing in the morning I'd get everything organized, go online to make payments, write checks where needed, and get everything squared away.*

Morning would come, I'd go to class and forget about my bills until the next night. Three months passed. Everything came to a head when the telephone company turned off my landline and my dad couldn't get hold of me at my apartment. He called me on my cell to tell me that my phone had been disconnected. I hadn't even noticed!

Dad was upset and got the whole story out of me in short order. I can't hold out on my dad. He told me to come home that weekend and bring all my bills with me.

We sat at the breakfast table. He told me to open all the envelopes, organize the bills by name, with the latest one on top. Then we looked at my online bills. It took a while. I sat quietly while he looked at everything. Then he turned to me, gave me a sad look, and said I'd probably ruined my credit rating. He was disappointed in me—he thought I was more responsible.

Later, Mom took me to lunch and talked to me about being responsible. She got my attention. She said, "Alan, you've always procrastinated—we've talked about this before. You put things off until later. But you've never had to manage your finances before, and now this behavior is affecting your life more significantly. You can choose to go through life this way, and believe me, it's your choice, or you can make changes. It's up to you. Think about the way you want to live your life. Do you want to live fully and in the moment, or do you want to drift—thinking about accomplishment, but delaying your action? You won't achieve nearly as much that way, which is not what I want for you, but it's your choice. You decide."

My parents hadn't talked to me in such a strong way before. *I shaped up for a while—opening and paying my bills on time, but then I slid back into my old habits. I was busy and thought I'd take care of the bills later. But my mother's warning words about my procrastination worried me. She was right. And it hurt that she felt that way about me. I realized I not only put off paying bills but I put off a lot of things.*

I didn't return phone calls promptly and sometimes not at all. Class reading assignments were done just before the test or quiz. Term papers were completed in a panic at the last moment and often turned in late. I avoided meeting with my counselor to discuss my future career plans.

I began to grasp what Mom meant by living life fully. If I didn't jump in and get things done, I'd just sit around thinking about doing them. And that meant I never moved on to other possibilities. I was letting the little tasks of living paralyze me.

I had to change. *It didn't happen overnight. Even though I've been working on not procrastinating for several years, I still have this tendency to put responsibilities off. But I've learned to handle them. For example, I open all my mail and email every day, and I pay my bills as soon as I receive them. I know I might earn a few cents in interest if I paid* them when they're due, but it works better for me to write a check or pay online as soon as I open the bill. That way, bill paying isn't such a big job, and it helps make me feel on top of things. Anytime I can get the payment automatically deducted from my checking account, like my car lease or cable, I arrange that.

As far as term papers and reading assignments went, I developed a "head start" regimen on projects. I started to read textbooks before classes began. That way, I stayed ahead of the assignments. I felt more confident in my studies, learned more, and enjoyed my classes. My grades improved too. It was difficult for me to figure out how to get term papers finished on schedule, so I started on the paper as soon as I got the assignment and set aside time every day to work on it. My energy level stayed up when I made steady progress on the assignment. Most of all, I was filled with a sense of success when I finished it on time.

Now that I'm in the work world, these same techniques help me get proposals and reports together in a timely fashion. My methods may sound simplistic, but since I've never figured out why I procrastinate, I can only find ways to circumvent the tendency. I haven't solved all my problems, but the more I create systematic ways to complete tasks, the better I deal with this trait.

Besides paying my bills on time, I learned to check my bank balance and review charges in my account. I know some people say that's not necessary anymore since banking is computerized and there is little chance of a bank error. But once in a while, a debit charge didn't show up for a couple of days so I learned that my balance online might not be accurate, that I would need to be sure to have enough money in checking.

But I discovered another reason to periodically review my checking account. It helps me think about the past week, look at how I spent my money, and consider my future money issues. Do I want to buy a piece of furniture, add to my retirement account, or go on vacation this winter? The act of sitting at my desk and reviewing my accounts centers me around my money—gives me a sense of being in control.

For a while, I also matched up my credit card receipts with the listing on the statement, but I decided that was too much work. Now I check my account online several times a week, and if something looks off or I don't remember it, I check my folding file for the receipt or I call the credit card company for more information.

I've never had an incorrect billing on my credit card bill, but I have seen things I wasn't expecting. Once I was out of town for a couple weeks and I made my credit card payment a day after the payment deadline. They charged me an $84 late fee. I called the credit-card company and asked for forgiveness, and they removed the charge for that one time but cautioned me to mail the payment before the due date in the future.

I didn't realize I was paying a $90 annual fee after the first year for my credit card. That charge showed up on the statement at the end of twelve months. The information about the annual fee was buried in the application form I signed for the card, which I didn't read carefully. I decided to keep the card—I collect air miles for every dollar I charge—but now I want to know what I'm paying for. Before, anything could have shown up on my credit card and I'd have paid it.

I wish I'd started managing my finances before college. *If so, I might not have gotten so out of control my first time away from home. Once I focused on my issues of procrastination with money and changed my behavior regarding finances, I applied the same principles to other areas of my life. I developed better relationships with friends. I became more confident. I didn't waste time. My grades improved. I met with a counselor and set my career path in motion. And I proved to myself and my parents that I could take control of my life.*

PROCRASTINATION

It's so easy to put off financial matters. Sitting down to pay bills each month is difficult for a lot of people. Some of my clients describe getting cold sweats or feeling dread at the prospect of writing those checks and making online payments. It might also stem from the reluctance to give up cash sitting in the bank. At any rate, you cannot afford to delay paying your bills. You need to find ways to make it less painful and more automatic. Alan's idea of paying a bill as soon as it arrives in the mail makes sense if you have the money in checking. That way, you are usually only paying one or two bills; it's quicker and takes barely any of your time. If you are living paycheck to paycheck, pay bills every time you receive your pay.

Your bank may offer bill-paying options using your personal computer or smartphone. Financial apps like Mint will alert you when a bill is coming due. Certain businesses will agree to automatically deduct the monthly payment directly from your checking account or charge your credit card. Automatic deductions are handy for those fixed monthly payments like rent, insurance, or a car payment.

Ask for Help

If you're having trouble dealing with procrastination, ask your friends, a parent, or trusted advisor if they have any ways of dealing with this issue. Maybe they have a solution that feels right for you.

OPEN YOUR MAIL

Alan said he didn't open his mail regularly. Opening your mail and email is the first step to taking responsibility for your financial life.

While interviewing people about what they had learned about money, one graduate proudly told me he'd finally paid off all his credit card debt in three years after graduation. But then he got a big surprise. He never bothered to open the monthly bank statements or review his checking account online. One day he got a phone call from a clerk at a local bookstore telling him his debit charge was returned for insufficient funds. Puzzled, he quickly looked at his bank statements and was shocked to discover that he'd been regularly overdrawing his account. He had overdraft protection for his checking account, so the bank had covered previous purchases but he had exceeded the limit on the overdraft account and the bank would not cover the check to the bookstore.

Bankers tell me customers often use overdraft protection as though it were a credit card, but the real purpose is to protect debit charges and checks being returned for insufficient funds. Overdraft protection is a useful money-management tool. Use it as intended.

OVERDRAFT PROTECTION

If you request overdraft protection, the bank will cover overdrafts by charging an account set up for this purpose. The bank establishes a line of credit based on your request—maybe $200 to $1,000. Any overdrafts in checking are funded by this account. Information about overdrafts appear on the monthly bank statement along with a request to pay at least a minimum amount on the overdraft account, just like a credit card. If the client doesn't pay, the bank automatically deducts the minimum monthly payment from checking and charges interest on the unpaid balance.

If you don't qualify for overdraft protection, see if your bank will link your checking account to your savings. If you overdraw checking, the bank can transfer funds from savings. There will probably be a fee for this service. Or you may opt for a notification text from your bank when your account drops to a certain level. Ask if your bank has this service.

Overdraft protection and these other methods are a safety net. We all make mistakes from time to time, like forgetting a debit charge or an ATM withdrawal. With overdraft protection, you can be assured of avoiding expensive charges for bad checks and debit charges. Make a promise to yourself that you will always pay off any charges to your overdraft account in the month you receive your bank statement. If you treat this service like a credit card where you carry a balance owed, you risk exceeding your limit and the bank will not cover your check. A returned payment is embarrassing and expensive. The bank will charge a fee, and many creditors also charge a customer for a bounced payment. You could end up paying $50 to $70 for one bad check or debit purchase, not to mention the time you will spend getting everything straightened out.

MORE THAN MONEY

Alan discovered something significant—a sense of order in one's life and taking charge. The tendency to delay doing the things in life that must be done depletes energy. If you take charge of your financial life, you'll find that other parts of your existence will improve too. For many people, the art of maintaining a systematic financial life seems too hard, so they don't bother. As a result, other parts of their existence take on disorder too. Alan found simple ways to stay on top of his finances, and in doing so he was rewarded in many ways. His approach to schoolwork changed and his grades improved. His friends no longer perceived him as irresponsible. Oftentimes we think change requires massive, groundbreaking steps. But Alan made small, simple changes to improve. You can too.

KEY TAKEAWAYS

- Open your mail and email every day.
- Pay your bills on time or, if you tend to procrastinate, pay them when you receive the bill.
- Use the option of moving a due date in a billing cycle to match with dates of incoming funds or paychecks.
- Check out automatic bill paying or online banking.
- Review financial management apps and pick one that will work for you.
- If you have certain bills automatically paid each month, be sure to enter the payment on your accounts register so you don't inadvertently overdraft your account.
- Run automatic payments through your credit card so that you don't have to worry about bank overdrafts.
- Talk with your banker or go to your bank's website to find out about options for some kind of overdraft protection or balance notification.
- Review the potential bank fees and charges for returned checks, overdrafts, automatic transfers, and any other service fees. You can find this at the bank's website or in written materials given to you when you set up the account.

11

Now Where Did I Put That?

TIM'S STORY

I've always used the "pile" system. At any one time I have four to six piles of papers on my desk. One pile for coming events and concerts, one for class assignments, one or more piles for term papers I am working on, one for all the graduate school information I'm collecting, one for my bills and other financial stuff. You get the idea. This system always worked for me when I was at home. When I went to college, I didn't give any thought to changing my system. Boy, was I wrong! I got seriously messed up and messed with because of my sloppy methods.

I remember bragging *to my new roommates my system worked and I always knew where everything was. Of course, my desk looked like a disaster, but I was on top of things. I have a good memory and could always remember which pile I put something in. Just to be sure, though, every once in a while, I'd go through one of my piles to refresh my memory about what was there and restack the papers in a neat pile.*

This method was working pretty well at college until one warm autumn day. One of my roommates needed fresh air, opened all the windows, and left for class. A wind gusted through the room. It took hours to pick up all the papers and sort them out again. My roommates thought it was hilarious and kidded me about my system. I decided to "secure" my files by collecting heavy rocks I set on top of each pile of papers.

Life went on. *I was happy to be in college, enjoyed my classes, and had a good social life. My roommates and I had a lot of friends who dropped into our room. Our dorm was a happening place, and I liked the action even if I didn't always know the visitors.*

All my financial stuff was in one pile: student loan information, credit card and telephone numbers in case I lost one and had to report it, PINs, passwords, bank statements, checkbook, a box of blank checks, paid and unpaid bills, and a debit card that I didn't use very often.

My parents paid my tuition and half the room and board. They wanted me to begin to learn how to manage my money, so they made a monthly deposit into my checking account of a portion of the money I needed for the year. It was up to me to make sure I kept track of what I'd need to pay next semester's expenses and tuition, and set aside part of the funds for these future bills. I was good at this. I never was a big spender and didn't feel tempted to spend all my cash. I made a note in my checkbook every month about how much money I was saving for next semester and I didn't add that amount into the balance that I was using on a day-to-day basis.

As classes got more demanding, *I got busier. I quit reviewing my banking activity. It wasn't a big deal. I knew I wouldn't run out of funds because I had quite a bit of money in checking. I planned to check my account between semesters.*

Just before I went home for break, I used my smartphone to make payments to the university for the next semester's tuition and dorm fees. I still hadn't looked at my checking account, but I wasn't concerned. I was sure there was enough money to cover the fees.

After I got home, I got a notice from the university that my payments had been returned for insufficient funds. I would be denied admission for the next semester. I was in shock. There had to be some mistake—a screw up by the bank. I called the bank and they told me I had $1,200 in checking. I thought I had over $10,000! The banker suggested I review my statements. Perhaps a deposit wasn't made or I made an error in addition.

I started balancing my checking account with the bank statements. September checked out fine. All the October deposits were there, just as my parents had promised. The funny thing was that under the section showing cleared checks was a check number that was way out of sequence. I hardly ever wrote checks, but I'd started with number 100. This check was number 142, and it was for a large amount—$2,200. I thought maybe the bank charged someone else's check against my account. In November and December, the same thing happened. Three more checks appeared out of sequence—143, 144, and 145—all written for $2,200 each. A total of $8,800 had been deducted from my checking account. Checks I hadn't written!

I immediately called the bank. When I told them I hadn't written the four checks, they said they'd order a copy of each check and send them to me.

In the meantime, I called the Fee Collection office and talked with the manager. I explained the situation and asked her if there was anything I could do. She said I needed to get my fees paid in full, plus pay late-fee penalties by Monday or I wouldn't be admitted for next term. She suggested I have the bank wire the money to the Fee Collection office or pay over the phone with a credit card. I didn't have a big enough credit line to handle the fees. I told her I'd get back to her.

I decided I'd better tell my parents what was going on. They said they'd pay my fees with their credit card if I'd agree to review my banking information with them.

The copies of the four checks came two days later. They looked like my checks. My name was signed on the signature line, but it wasn't my signature. I couldn't figure out what had happened, until my dad asked me where I kept my blank checks. I told him they were in my financial pile. He asked if this pile was locked up. I told him the story about the heavy rock on the top of the pile.

He explained about stolen blank checks. Often the thief takes checks from the back of the book so that the loss won't be noticed right away. Obviously, someone had opened the box of blank checks on top of my desk, stolen checks, and forged my signature. Dad thought we'd be able to get the money back from the bank—they could honor only my signature—but we'd better notify them immediately.

The bank said they'd compare the signature on the forged checks to the signature card I signed when I opened the account. In the meantime, they told me to report the theft to the campus police. The police officer said she would file a report, and when I returned to campus, I should come to their office to make a complete statement.

I couldn't believe one of my roommates would forge checks. Dad said if I left my blank checks out in plain view, anyone could be tempted. I told *him we had a lot of visitors, some of them strangers to me. It was time for me to lock up my checks.*

Dad said he thought I'd better rethink my "pile" system, too. *Not just checks. Certain items need to be protected, such as PINs, social security number, credit and debit card numbers, and bank statements. Everything must be locked in a safe place.*

I got everything straightened out with the bank and the university, and I returned to class for the next term. The police investigated, but they never caught anyone. They published a notice in the student newspaper warning other students of the potential problem. I was glad. I'd never heard of such a thing—stolen blank checks and forged signatures on a college campus. If I'd known, I might have been more careful. I felt lucky. Things got settled without too much financial loss to me. And no one stole my credit card, social security card, or my identity.

I still operate on a pile system, but all my financial and personal information stays locked up.

PROTECT SENSITIVE MATERIALS

Your dorm room is not the most private or secure place you could live, so you need to exercise a little more care in protecting your financial assets from theft or inquisitive people.

Blank checks are sensitive documents and need to be treated as if they were cash. Tim's story highlights one of the reasons checking accounts need to be reviewed regularly. He would have caught the problem months earlier and saved a lot of anxious moments and time.

You probably don't write checks very often, but when you do, it's a good idea to jot down the number, name, and amount in the check register that came with your blank checks. That way you'll notice a missing consecutively numbered check and can call your bank or access your account online to see if the check has cleared your account. You may have written a check and neglected to record it. Ask the bank for the name of the payee and the amount. Or, your online bank records may have an image of the cancelled check. If you've written the check, this information will probably jog your memory. If you're sure you haven't written the check, notify the bank immediately. If the check hasn't cleared the bank, you can stop payment on the check so that it will not be charged against your account. There'll probably be a fee for this service. If the check has already cleared, pull the check from your bank statement, or if your bank doesn't return checks, ask the bank to send a copy.

TAKE ACTION

Always notify the appropriate people and organizations. Tim called the bank and the university. He notified the police in the jurisdiction where the theft took place. Then he asked for help. This isn't a time to put things off and hope everything will work out. You need to attack the issue and get it straightened out. If you don't know what to do, ask someone you trust to help or check with the appropriate officials at the university.

Sometimes the little things in life defeat us. Tim was proud of his pile system, but it had its drawbacks: spending precious time sifting through piles of paper looking for a particular item, turning a room upside down looking for an important article needed for a paper, or forgetting to pay a bill because it's in the wrong pile or slipped in between the pages of a magazine. Not only do we lose time and get discouraged, we can adversely affect our credit history by not having a system.

To some people, the words "having a system" seem like too much work, but you can create a simple and efficient method as you start your financial life. Simple systems enable you to save time, energy, and negative emotions. Secure, organized files allow you to rest a little easier knowing your financial information is protected.

WHAT DOCUMENTS SHOULD BE SAVED

The following list will guide you on what to save and for how long:

- Your birth certificate, social security card, passport, marriage license, and divorce papers. Keep these forever.

- Tax returns. Keep the filled-out forms, W-2s, and 1099s in a permanent file. Any supporting documentation (you probably will not have any as a student) can be thrown out after three years. Keep supporting documents and tax forms for seven years if you have a more complicated return.
- Student-loan agreements, student financial aid notices, statements, and correspondence. Keep for the life of the loan.
- Other loan agreements, lease contracts such as a car. Keep for the life of the loan or lease.
- Credit card paperwork that includes the card number and a toll-free number to call in case it is lost or stolen. This information usually is sent with the credit card. Keep for as long as you have the credit card.
- Credit card statements. Keep for one year. If you receive online statements, your credit card company will probably keep the statements available for several years.
- Bank statements for checking and savings accounts, and canceled checks (if your bank returns them to you—most provide the information online). Keep for one year. You may have opted to receive online statements so you won't have to maintain a paper file—the bank will keep your statements.
- Receipts for important items. Keep for one year except for items under warranty.
- Warranties for your computer or other items covered. Keep for the life of the warranty.
- Insurance policies. Keep as long as the policy is active.

STORAGE OPTIONS

That's a formidable list at first glance. What's the best way to keep this information? There are several ways to handle this. You could buy a small filing cabinet or a cardboard file box and make folders for all these items. If you enjoy keeping records in this way, go ahead. But as a college student, you will not have a huge amount of information to keep on file, so an easy way to keep it all in one place is to buy a large three-ring binder and plastic envelope inserts. As you receive documents that need to be saved, slide them in the plastic envelopes. This way, you can leaf through your notebook and quickly retrieve what you are looking for. This works particularly well for loan documents, insurance policies, birth certificate, passport, and so on—papers you'll be keeping for a while or forever. You may want to keep everything in this file or you may decide that bank statements, credit card statements and receipts—items you'll throw out in a year or so—can go in an expanding file. You can throw them away at the end of a year and reuse the file.

If you're concerned about the security of certain permanent documents, rent a safe-deposit box at your bank. Or keep them in a fire-resistant lockbox that you can put out of sight. Another better option is to keep most of this information at home in a safe place.

If you're using a personal accounting app, be sure to back up your data regularly. It's time consuming to recreate a financial history.

Whatever system you use, make sure it's secure—that it can be locked up and not easily seen by others. A desk drawer with a lock is fine if you are using the binder system. And be sure to lock up your blank checks and information on your PINs.

Give your parents a copy of your vital information so they have a back-up copy in case of an emergency.

IDENTITY THEFT

There's growing concern about identity theft. Never reveal your social security number unless there's a good reason for using it, like on your tax return or bank account application. Do not use your social security card as identification. If you receive a call from someone purporting to represent your bank or university and asking for your social security number or other sensitive data, you can be pretty sure it is a scam. Instead, ask them for their name, phone number, and extension number, and tell them you'll call back.

When you throw away credit card receipts or statements, make sure your account number is obliterated by inking out the number and tearing the receipt or shredding these papers. People have been known to go through trash looking for active credit card numbers. You may opt to go strictly online for your statements and won't need to worry about paper documents getting into the wrong hands.

Be cautious when inputting your PIN for debit card purchases. Protect your information by blocking the pad with your hand and your body. Don't write down your PIN number in an obvious place like a pad on your desk or keep the number in your wallet along with the debit card. If you lose your wallet, you could lose your entire checking account balance.

If your wallet is lost or stolen, notify your bank and credit card companies of debit and credit card losses. Go one step further. Notify the three national credit-reporting organizations to place a fraud alert on your name and social security number:

1. Equifax: (800) 525-6285, www.alerts.equifax.com
2. Experian: (888) 397-03742, www.experian.com
3. TransUnion: (800) 680-7289, www.transunion.com

It's a good idea to order a credit report annually. You can get a free credit report once a year at www.AnnualCreditReport.com. If someone has opened a charge or credit card account using your name without your knowledge, you'll see it on the report. There have been instances where accounts have been opened with a new mailing address so that the responsible person isn't aware of charges building in their name. The monthly bill never reaches the responsible party, and the identity thieves continue racking up debt in another's name.

As I was preparing this revised edition, I continued to follow my regular practice of reviewing my credit card transactions every few days. Three charges for $42.25, $211.50, and $312.75 appeared one morning under *pending items.* I didn't recognize the company name, checked with my husband, who confirmed he hadn't purchased anything from this company, and called the credit card company to see what they could tell me. They gave me the phone number of the company, and I called them. It turns out someone had used my husband's name and credit card number to open an account with this company. The address, phone number, and social security number given were not his. The company agreed the charges were fraudulent, and I called back the credit card company with this information. They immediately cancelled our compromised card and sent a new one that arrived two days later. They also put a fraud alert on our account with Experian. The bogus charges were erased from our bill, and the credit card company was responsible for recovering any payments from the company who accepted the fake information.

KEY TAKEAWAYS

- Develop a simple system to pay bills and for storage of vital information.
- Review your bank and credit card statement at least once a week.
- Always sign your checks the same as the bank signature card you signed when you opened your account.
- Never give out your credit card number or social security number over the phone or via email to a stranger who contacts you.
- If you notice a discrepancy on any financial statements, or if something is lost or stolen, immediately notify the appropriate institution.

After College

12

What's Next?

GABE'S STORY

What a relief! I was finally done with college and had a great job lined up. My starting salary with a software firm was competitive with the possibility of a year-end bonus, and I got a signing bonus. I didn't even have to move to another town. I was feeling very prosperous until my older brother, Roth, had a chat with me.

He warned me *not to take the same missteps he'd taken. He said he never told anyone about his problems because he was so embarrassed, but he was telling me because he thought it might save me from making the same mistakes.*

Roth felt on top of the world when he graduated from college. He had some student loans and had been careful not to accumulate credit card debt, but when he graduated and landed a good job, he felt rich and quickly bought a new car, purchased expensive clothes, found a great apartment, and hired a decorator to furnish it. With a bright future ahead, he thought he needed to look the part.

With his new salary, Roth thought he could easily manage, so he charged everything he wanted on his credit cards. Premium cable, fine restaurants, a fancy athletic club, business lunches, a new tablet, and the latest smartphone racked up huge credit card debt.

Reality surfaced when he got his first paycheck. His take-home pay was a third lower than he expected. He'd forgotten about payroll taxes and health insurance premiums that would be withheld from his check.

Roth had to backpedal real fast in order to stay afloat financially. He returned the unworn clothes, stopped the decorator in mid-job, and sold the new car at a loss and got a used one. Even so, in just one month he'd racked up $20,000 in credit card debt that would take a couple of years to pay off. Money worries kept him awake at night, and he no longer enjoyed all the things he had accumulated.

After hearing his story, *I was grateful to have someone help me work out a financial plan for my first year. I knew it'd be foolish not to take advantage of my brother's knowledge.*

The first thing I did was contact the human resources office of my new company to determine my take-home pay amount from the monthly salary and the signing bonus. Knowing my monthly cash income helped settle me into my financial status as a young professional, and I felt confident about my prospects and myself.

Roth asked me to make a wish list *of everything I wanted to buy. That was awesome. I wanted a sports car, a bigger apartment, new living-room furniture, a European vacation, a skiing trip to Aspen, and a big-screen TV. I knew I couldn't afford it all, but it was cool fantasizing.*

Roth told me to write each item and its cost on a 3x5 index card, look them over during the next few weeks, put them in order of importance, and make up new cards for any other things that came to mind. I laid the cards out on my desk and prioritized and then reprioritized. Every time I walked by my desk, I stopped and looked at the cards. My wish list cards helped me think about what was most important to me. Since I was also preparing a list of all my basic living expenses at the same time, I began to think about alternatives to my expensive items. Were there things on the list that I wanted that could be fulfilled in other ways? How long was I willing to wait for a particular item?

Two weeks later I had my prioritized list, my take-home pay, and my budget for basic expenses. Roth handed me a worksheet, and I filled in the blanks. My finances looked good, and I was still planning that skiing trip when Roth asked me if I'd signed up for the company's 401(k) plan. I hadn't, thinking I'd put it off for a while until I got settled financially. Roth persuaded me to sign up immediately.

The company matched my contributions up to 3% of my salary. For *every dollar I put in, the company put in another dollar. As Roth pointed out, this was like getting a raise my first month. Not only that but the money deposited in the 401(k) was tax-deferred, meaning I didn't have to pay income taxes on it until I withdrew it, so I would be investing my taxes and earning money on them until I retired.*

When my brother first started talking about retirement, I thought he was way off base. That's so far from my priorities now. But he told me the earlier I started putting away retirement money, the less I'd have to worry about saving in the future because the markets will have more time to grow my investments. Roth said it would give me more freedom in the future, and if I started paying in now, I'd never miss the money. I wasn't so sure about that, but I trusted his advice and signed up for the retirement plan. Why pass up free money?

As we worked on my spending plan, I continued to revise my wish list and made some decisions. I decided to stay in my apartment for at least another year. I liked the place, and the price was right. I put half the signing bonus into savings to set up my emergency fund. I treated myself to a nice leather armchair, a new TV, and a down payment for a used car.

It's been five years since I graduated from college. I'm so thankful I listened to my older brother. As time went on, I received salary increases, built my savings and investments, and bought things on my wish list that I still wanted. I don't have any credit card debt. I am especially proud of that because I have several friends who have huge credit card debt and lose sleep worrying about it. Roth saved me from money missteps, and last year, to pay him back, I took him to Aspen with me.

LOOK TO THE FUTURE

The very first thing you do after accepting a new job is sign up for your organization's retirement program and, if possible, put the maximum amount allowed into the plan. At the very least allocate enough to earn the company's matching percentage. And promise yourself you'll increase the contribution as you receive raises. Don't worry about not having enough money to live on—you *will* adjust to your take-home pay. Remember you'll be bringing in a lot more money than you had in college. If you've been careful not to accumulate expensive credit card debt and kept your student loans in check, you will not have any trouble living on the new salary, minus the retirement contributions.

You may be tempted to wait to start your retirement planning. After all, you're young, and you have many years before you will actually retire. It may seem counterintuitive to worry about an event that's forty years away. Look at it this way. Assume you want $1,000,000 when you are sixty-five. If you start saving at age eighteen, earning a 10% annual return, you'll need to save $78 a month. If you wait until you're twenty-five to start saving, you'll need to put away $170 a month. At thirty-five, you'll need $442, and at forty-five, your savings will have to be $1,317 a month in order to reach your goal of $1,000,000 at age sixty-five. The earlier you start saving, the less you'll have to invest over time because your money is working for you, growing and adding to your retirement savings. This is an example of the power of compound interest.

If your new employer doesn't have a retirement plan, go to your bank or a financial services company and ask them to set up an Individual Retirement Account (IRA) for you. The Khan Academy (www.khanacademy.org) has free informative short videos on 401(k) plans and IRAs. Check them out.

Every month, have the financial institution automatically transfer one-twelfth of the maximum amount you can contribute from your checking account into your new IRA account. Investing in an index fund (either a mutual fund or exchange traded fund) when you're young will be beneficial because this money will be invested for many years, and experience has shown us that the stock market produces the best return over the long term. You can look for target-date mutual funds. Let's suppose you think you'll retire in 2060. You can buy a mutual fund that is managed to optimize your money, aiming for the year 2060.

COVER YOURSELF

You'll need to make decisions on other benefits offered by your employer. In addition to signing up for medical insurance with your new organization, be sure to apply for disability insurance, if it's offered. Long-term disability insurance is especially important for the young, because if the unthinkable happens, a person needs to have supplemental income that will last a lifetime. In other words, if you were paralyzed in an auto accident and unable to earn enough money to be independent, disability insurance could fill the gap, give you financial security, and reduce the stress of inadequate funds over your lifetime, which could be more than fifty years.

COST OF LIVING

Draw up a new spending plan. It'll have two components: the monthly or regular costs to live—rent, insurance, transportation, entertainment, utilities, food, student-loan payments, renter's insurance—and the one-time costs for starting a new life. These one-time costs may include a deposit on a new apartment, moving expenses, a new wardrobe, a car down payment, furniture, outfitting a kitchen, and other household items. These costs can mount quickly and may seem overwhelming. Remember, knowledge is power, and if you have this information down in writing where you can review it, you're more likely to make rational decisions with your money and avoid debt.

It will be to your benefit and long-term financial security to start out slowly on your spending when you begin your career. Promise yourself you will live a lifestyle beneath your income rather than the one you wish you had. By living below your means, you can accumulate funds for investing, a home, or other assets. Don't think of this as a restriction; consider it a way, in the long run, to create options for the way you live your life.

Give yourself some time to experience your new costs of living. Then adjust your plan as you learn more. It's difficult to cut back later when you start out spending more money than you earn. Some people rationalize the shortfall. They start borrowing on credit cards, believing that they can make up the deficit after the next raise or bonus. That kind of thinking is a guaranteed path to a lifetime of debt.

MONTHLY SAVINGS AND EMERGENCY FUNDS

Remember to build in a monthly amount to be saved in your spending plan. This is in addition to your retirement contribution. Initially, use the savings to build an emergency fund of three to six months of living expenses. Emergency funds give you financial security in the event you're not earning an income or you have some unexpected expenses. This could happen if your company goes under or downsizes. Or you might be injured and need medical treatment not covered by insurance. Or you're required to relocate, and your company does not fully cover the costs of moving.

The emergency fund should be held in a savings or money market account. It may not pay much interest, but you want the money to be risk-free and to be able to access the cash immediately in an emergency. After you are satisfied with the amount in the emergency fund, continue your savings program and allocate your money to other longer-term investments, such as certificates of deposit (CDs), treasury bills, corporate or tax-free bonds, and stock funds. Begin to educate yourself on the financial markets and investment world by reading newspapers such as the *Wall Street Journal,* or attending a class or seminar. Many financial institutions give free seminars on various financial topics, and educational institutions offer classes through their continuing education divisions. Look for online programs that will allow you to gather information at your own pace.

STUDENT LOANS

A common question from new graduates: should I pay off my student loans as soon as possible, or should I pay the minimum monthly amount and save and invest the money? The best approach is to follow what's outlined above, especially funding your 401(k) and saving enough to fund three to six months of emergency funds. Then step back and re-evaluate your financial situation. You'll have had some months of experience with your new life and will feel more confident in your decisions. Make sure your spending plan is realistic. How much money do you have left over each month? If you add this money to your monthly loan repayment, how long will it take you to pay off your loans? Are you willing to take that long without saving and investing some more money? You may decide you want to get the loans behind you. You may decide you'll feel more secure if you save part of the money and pay down loans with the rest. You may decide to stay with the regular loan payment each month and save more money.

The answer to the question about paying off student loans early is: it depends. It depends on your financial personality and what makes you most comfortable. If you decide to accelerate your loan payments, take your list of student loans, prioritize them starting with the loans with the highest interest rate. If you accelerate payments, it makes sense to pay off the most expensive loans first.

But here's one more thing to consider. Starting to save when you're young is so beneficial. Time is your friend. Let's suppose you have $200 a month that can either be applied to student loans or saved. If you start saving $200 a month when you're twenty-two and continue until you're sixty-five, you will have invested a total of $103, 200. If you earn an average 10% annual return over those forty-three years, your savings will grow to $1,713,558. If you decide to wait until your student loans are paid and start investing the $200 a month at age thirty-two, your investment at sixty-five will be $79,200, and your account will have grown to $617,866. If you want to consider other scenarios, go to www.financialcalculator.org and use their compound interest calculator.

Overwhelmed by Student Loan Payments

You've got a job but the cost of living is higher than you expected or your salary is too low to cover all your basic living expenses. You're losing sleep over your finances. What are your options?

Pull out your master list of student loans and then double check your information at the National Student Loan Data System website (www.nslds.ed.gov) to make sure you haven't missed a loan and to confirm who the servicer is on each loan.

Most federal student loans are based on a ten-year repayment schedule, but you may be able to extend the schedule as long as thirty years. One way to do this is to consolidate all your loans into a single one. Or you may be able to enroll in a graduated payment program where your monthly payments will increase over time when you are making a larger salary and more able to make a bigger payment. Check out the Student Loan Borrower Assistance Project of the National Consumer Law Center (www.student-loanborrowerassistance.org) for a guide to loan consolidation.

If you are not making much income, you may qualify for a government program that will base your payments on how much money you make. Go to the Department of Education's main income-based repayment web page (www.studentaid.ed.gov/sa/repay-loans/understand/plans/income-driven) for current information. Your servicer will determine if you qualify for reduced payments. Under certain circumstances, the federal government may eventually forgive the debt. Talk to your servicer about your options.

If you have private loans, contact the lender and ask what you can do to reduce the monthly payments.

If you do extend your loans, remember that you'll be paying more interest over time. The example of how much money you can accumulate if you start saving early works in reverse when it comes to debt.

The most important aspect of all of this is to act quickly when you realize you cannot make the payments. If you skip or reduce a payment without talking to your servicer or lender, your credit history could be compromised, and a bad credit history will cost you more in interest when you take out a consumer loan or may make you unable to borrow money later on. If you decide to go to graduate school, you may be denied admission if you are considered in default on your student loans. It's always best to immediately contact a creditor when you cannot make the minimum payment and make other arrangements.

WISH LIST CARDS

You may have more start-up costs than money as you start your new career. Before you take on debt to fund these costs, do what Gabe did on his brother's advice. Write down each potential purchase on an index card. Play with the cards for a few weeks;

arrange them in the order of most importance to you. New ideas may come to mind as you review the cards. For example, you may decide to get along without a car for a year or buy a used car instead of a new one. Write down these new ideas on cards and see how those changes affect your thinking. But be honest with yourself. If a new car is of the utmost importance, then figure out how you can get it within your income. It may mean giving up other things, and if you decide you can do that, go for it!

Pay attention to needs versus wants. Separate the cards into these categories and consider your financial nature. Think through how to manage the wants in a way that will satisfy you but not lead to overspending. Look at the cards in terms of short- and long-term wants. Are you the type of person who can wait to acquire some wants? Or is the acquisition energy difficult to resist? These are clues to your financial nature, and the first step in managing wants is to recognize the kind of instincts you have around money. We don't all handle money in the same way. Once you understand yourself, you can begin to manage your money in a way that works for you.

OTHER NEEDS FOR A NEW LIFE

Be sure you understand the prevailing dress climate in your work environment before you buy a new wardrobe. I remember a young assistant professor starting her first teaching job at a prestigious university. She was advised that business suits were appropriate only to find out once she had purchased five new suits that none of the other professors dressed that way. She spent $3,000 on clothing that could've been used for other purposes.

One way to assemble a less expensive work wardrobe is to shop at resale shops that specialize in top quality clothing or look for discount clothing on the Internet. After you have a basic wardrobe, you can shop sales to add other items.

If you need furniture, check with your relatives. Maybe someone has an attic full of things that you could borrow or use permanently. Look into buying used furniture by going to garage sales, auctions, or stores that handle used furniture. Perhaps you'll find a talent in refinishing pieces or learning how to reupholster a chair.

SOURCES OF FUNDS

Once you're certain of your immediate needs, what should you do if you still need extra money? Sometimes your firm will have a credit union. This may be your best source of money because credit unions usually offer slightly lower interest rates for car loans and personal loans to their members. However, you may have to be a member of the credit union for a certain number of months before taking out a loan. If a credit union loan is not possible, go to your bank and talk with them about getting a loan. Try not to fund your start-up costs using your credit card. It's just too expensive.

Perhaps your parents or grandparents would be willing to loan you money at the current bank rate. Draw up a simple contract with them stating:

1. Amount borrowed
2. Interest rate
3. Amount you'll pay each month on the loan
4. Due date of the monthly payment

You can create an amortization schedule for the loan by using a financial calculator or going to a website that has a calculator, such as www.bankrate.com. Honor the repayment schedule. You want to have a good credit rating with your relatives. You never know when you may need help in the future, and they'll be more likely to advance you money if you've shown your good intentions about repayment. On the other hand, if you think asking relatives for a loan will create tension in the family, don't do it. Look for other sources of funds. It's not worth the strain.

You'll know how much you can afford to repay on a loan because you've already drawn up a spending plan. Be sure to keep your total monthly loan payments, including student loans, at no more than 10% to 15% of your monthly take-home pay. If you find your monthly debt repayment approaching 20%, take steps to reduce your loans by cutting other expenses or taking a second job and paying more each month on your debt.

RETURN TO YOUR SPENDING PLAN

Monitor your expenses carefully during the first three or four months of your new professional life to see if your spending plan is on target. It's almost impossible to draw up an exact list of monthly expenditures, so you'll be fine-tuning your plan as you go along. Some people like to consistently watch their spending and keep detailed records. There are good apps to track finances. Google for the latest information and check reviews on an app before you select the best one for you.

FIND YOUR BEST WAY

You need to find your best way to manage your money. Not everyone manages money in the same way, but we all have to take responsibility for our financial life. The key to mastering your money is to find what works for you while staying within these financial boundaries:

- Paying bills on time
- Keeping debt within reason
- Living below your means
- Saving for the future

Not only do we not all manage finances the same way but we don't all *spend* money the same way. Pay attention to what's important to you and what is not. I have three children. One son buys fresh flowers every week for his home. He and his wife enjoy them and say it brings them pleasure. My daughter would never spend money on cut flowers. She considers that an extravagance and buys plants that don't have to be replaced. She would rather spend her money on books. My other son uses the public library for reading material. But all are right, and they knowingly make their decisions within their own financial parameters.

This diversity in spending is important to remember as you bring a life partner into your world. You want to give each other some financial freedom as you learn to live together so that one can buy fresh flowers every week and the other books. This may mean keeping your money separate and funding the common expenses by setting up a third checking account that you both contribute to based on your income. Another way to add freedom for individual needs is for each partner to have their own "kitty" that they can spend in any way they wish.

As you pay attention to your spending habits and desires, you'll begin to figure out your financial nature. The important thing is for you to knowingly make your choices. To be flexible and make changes when necessary. To live fully in the present but remain aware of the future. To master your finances today while at the same time saving and preparing for a secure future.

KEY TAKEAWAYS

- Figure out your take-home pay. Go to your company's human resources department for help if you're unsure.
- Make a list of one-time expenditures needed for your transition from school to work.
- Create a spending plan for your new life.
- Sign up for a retirement plan and try to put in the maximum or at least contribute enough to qualify for full matching funds from your company.
- Save for your emergency fund. Put this money in a savings or money market account.
- After your emergency account is fully funded, consider the best use of your monthly savings. Do you want to continue saving to buy some of the items on your wish list or accelerate student loan payments or save for a house down payment or create a stock portfolio? Decide what feels comfortable for you and begin the process.
- If you need relief on monthly payments for student loans, go to www.studentaid.ed.gov to check the current rules or call the financial aid office at your alma mater for advice. Make a decision on how to proceed and contact the appropriate offices to enact your plan.

13

Investment Basics

HAZEL'S STORY

When I signed up for my company's retirement plan, I was asked how I wanted the money invested. There were so many options—company stock, money market funds, stock and bond mutual funds. My company gave me a write-up of the type of funds, their performance records, and management fees, but I hardly knew where to start.

I talked with my dad. After the crash in '08, I was scared to invest in the stock market. But Dad said, over the long term, the stock market is a good place to invest. He pointed out that my retirement money would be invested for over forty years, so I could afford to hold tight through the inevitable ups and downs of the market, and my chances of a good return over time were much higher. Dad said the investors who rode out the '08 troubles recovered their losses in a little over five years, and then the market soared. He said it was the people who got scared and sold out who took the losses.

Investing can be complicated, *so I decided to keep it simple. Dad suggested I start with an index fund. I went to www.investinganswers.com to learn what an index fund is. I learned that an index mutual fund is invested identically to the related index. For example, Standard and Poor's 500 (S&P 500) tracks the market ups and downs using 500 stocks. A*

Standard and Poor index mutual fund buys the same stocks in the identical proportion as the S&P. Index mutual funds have lower management costs than other stock mutual funds because they don't have to analyze which stocks to buy; they just follow the proportions of whatever index they're modeling.

It seemed reasonable to me, and I wouldn't have to make any other decisions for the time being. As Dad pointed out, if I got interested in investing, I could learn more and begin to branch out on my picks. His birthday present to me that year was a year's subscription to Money Magazine. *I smiled when I opened the card, but I do read the magazine, and I'm beginning to better understand the basics of investing.*

STOCKS, BONDS, MUTUAL FUNDS

Todd Ihrig, a financial advisor in Arlington, Virginia, has a good description of stocks, bonds, and mutual funds:

> The two most common assets that investors use are stocks and bonds. A share of stock represents partial ownership in the underlying company. So, if you buy one share of ACME Inc., you actually own a small part of that business. If you buy a bond issued by ACME Inc., you are effectively lending money to the company and may earn interest on that loan.
>
> To simplify investing, the financial industry created mutual funds. A mutual fund pools money from many investors and buys a bunch of stocks or bonds. So, when you buy a share of a mutual fund, you own a small portion of all of the underlying stocks or bonds that the fund has purchased. Think of it as buying a bundle. It is kind of like choosing a radio station, Pandora, or iTunes channel to listen to. You choose the channel that has the genre of music you like, but the station or provider chooses the individual songs you hear.

- Stocks—represent ownership in a company
- Bonds—represent loaning the company money
- Mutual funds—many investors band together to buy stocks or bonds in many companies

Risk Assessment

You'll want to assess your ability to take risk. If you know you'll check the market every day to see how you're doing and will be anxious when the market declines, then start out with a small allocation to stocks, maybe 10% of your contribution. You may find as time goes on you are more comfortable with risk and can adjust your allocations.

You may decide that since you'll have this money invested for thirty or forty years, you'll ride out the changes in the market, believing that over time your investment will grow greater than in more conservative options. Don't obsess over your decision—you can always make changes in the types of investment in your 401(k) or other retirement plan.

One of my clients was a newly licensed orthopedic surgeon. After years of living a frugal life, he and his wife now had significant income. He was extremely risk adverse and insisted on putting his retirement plan money in certificates of deposit—bank instruments that pay interest and mature at a stated time. Over time, as he got more comfortable with investing, he decided to branch out and invest part of his funds in stocks.

Once you've thought about how much risk you're willing to take, look at the options provided in your plan. If you're considering mutual funds, there should be information on the type of funds available, such as the fund's mission, its growth over time, and fees charged. A good record doesn't guarantee the same results going forward, but it gives the investor an indicator of management performance. There are independent rating systems to help you decide. Morningstar is an organization that examines and reports on stock and bond mutual funds as well as other investment products. You can get basic information that is easily comparable among your options to help make a decision such as one, three, and five-year performance, fund costs, and a one- to five-star rating, five being the best. Morningstar information may be provided in your company's materials, or there may be other data available that make it easy to compare performance.

Diversification

One of the great advantages of mutual funds is that they provide diversification—the fund holds many companies' stocks or bonds, and that spreads the risk. Here's an investing cautionary tale about not diversifying.

When my older son went to college, we agreed I would pay his tuition and give him a monthly allowance for his basic expenses. He'd have to find a part-time job for extras. During his sophomore year, he found a good job at the university's hospital. Unbeknownst to me, he cut down on his academic schedule and worked full-time while I continued to pay his monthly allowance.

What he wanted to do was save up enough money to start investing in the stock market. He was an accounting major and president of his college's business fraternity. He was eager to get an early start at assembling a stock portfolio and wanted to impress his friends. And he wanted to make some money.

After he thought he had enough money (I later learned it was about $10,000), he went to a brokerage firm and was assigned to a young financial advisor. He got some very bad advice. First, he was never questioned about when he might need some or all of the money; secondly, the broker put the entire amount into one stock in a new company that was considered by some to have great potential. By the end of the first year, the stock price had plummeted and he had $1,200 left. My son was shocked by how quickly he lost most of his money.

What mistakes were made here? He wanted to start a stock portfolio, which was fine, but he was doing it blind, relying on an inexperienced financial advisor to guide him. This was his only money. He had no emergency fund. He had no funds set aside to help him move, find and furnish an apartment, and buy a car when he started his career in a few more years. If he wanted to learn about the stock market through actual investments, he could have first taken a course on the basics. He'd have learned the danger in putting all his money in one stock. He'd have learned to divvy up his money among a number of stocks to reduce risk. With $10,000, he could have purchased five or ten stocks in different economic sectors. He'd have learned that one does not hop in and out of the market; one expects to invest for a significant period of time. (I'm not addressing day trading here.) A stock portfolio isn't like a savings account where the money is secure and fully accessible. If he needed money during a time when the overall market was down, he'd have to sell at a loss. That's why it's so important to first establish an emergency fund where the money is held in a risk-free savings account.

A mutual fund automatically provides diversification—more than you could provide yourself buying individual stocks or bonds. And you're getting professional portfolio management through the fund—you don't have to pick individual investments.

If your 401(k) offers company stock as an investment option and you value diversification, you would not want to put all your contribution there unless there is no other option.

ROLLOVERS

It's a fact of life that people move around from company to company or leave to start their own business. If you find new employment, you can leave your 401(k) with the old company or you can roll it over, meaning you can have the funds transferred to your new company's retirement plan or you can set up an IRA account with a bank, brokerage, or mutual fund and transfer the funds to this account. It's best to consolidate your funds into one account. Over a lifetime in the working world, it's possible to lose track of small pots of money left in former employers' retirement funds. Also note that some plans do not allow transfer of the employer's contribution until a target time of employment has been met. This information will be in the plan document.

In general, you shouldn't take the cash from the plan—have the money transferred from one plan to the new one so that you never see the money. You could be liable for income taxes on the amount withdrawn plus a penalty for early withdrawal if you don't deposit the money in a new tax-deferred account within a certain time frame.

When one of my clients took a job in another state, he cashed out his retirement plan without consulting me. He deposited the $75,000 in his checking account and moved across the country to Oregon. In the meantime, his withdrawal, as required by federal law, was reported to the U.S. Treasury Department. He was busy with his new job and didn't line up a financial advisor or CPA until it was time to file his taxes. It was well past the sixty-day limit to transfer the funds to a new retirement account, and he was on the line for income taxes and penalties. His wife later told me they ended up paying about $25,000 in taxes and another $7,500 in penalties. They had lost $32,500 of their retirement money that should have remained invested and growing for another twenty years.

The easiest and safest way is to have the money or assets transferred between accounts—you never see the money. It will be reported as a rollover to the U.S. Treasury, and there won't be any danger of having to pay income taxes and penalties.

OTHER RETIREMENT PLANS

What if your employer does not offer a retirement plan or you are self-employed? You can still save for retirement by setting up an Individual Retirement Account (IRA) with a bank or brokerage firm or online mutual fund if you are earning a salary or making money from your own business.

The easiest and best way is to arrange for a monthly amount to be automatically withdrawn from your checking account and transferred to your investment account. Automatically investing each month is a terrific way of ensuring that your savings goal will be met. All you have to do is remember to deduct the monthly contribution from your checking account balance to prevent an overdraft.

WINDFALLS

Most people occasionally dream of getting an unexpected sum of money: winning the lottery, writing a best seller, receiving a generous signing bonus or an inheritance from a long-lost relative. It's thrilling to think of how the money could be spent to improve life and add enjoyment and peace of mind. A windfall can put a person into an excited acquisitive state. But think of the lottery winners who have gone broke after a few years or the NFL and NBA athletes who were paid millions for a short career and in retirement claim bankruptcy. Caution is advised.

Maybe it was because I grew up in Ohio, but I remember a story in the *New York Times* about Boomer Esiason's first season as a professional quarterback with the Cincinnati Bengals. He signed a three-year contract in June 1984 and received an immediate $600,000 signing bonus and three months later his entire first year's pay of $275,000. Remember this is 1984 dollars. In today's world it's the equivalent of at least $3.5 million, and that doesn't count salary inflation in professional sports.

By April he had $4,000 left and had to borrow money to get through the second season. According to the news article, he made two basic mistakes that many make when getting a windfall: he bought anything he wanted—a Rolex, a house for his dad and one for himself, jewelry for his girlfriend, a car, nice clothes—and he neglected to plan for how much taxes he would owe.

If you receive some unexpected money, don't go out and buy a new car the next day. Sit on this good luck, allow reason to take over, and think about what's important now and for your future.

You might try using the 3x5 card method I discussed in the previous chapter. I used this method with a client who became a multimillionaire overnight when the firm where she was a partner was acquired. Anne's biggest fear was that she would fritter away this unexpected bonanza.

She spent several months playing with options like retiring, sending her niece and nephews to graduate school, and buying a jazz club. She ultimately decided to continue working for the new firm, bought some finery (her word for new clothes), reassured her aging mother that she would provide for her, and became a partner in a jazz club. She said the cards gave her a good fix on what was really important to her.

If you've received a substantial amount of money, consider consulting a professional to help you plan how to use the money. A seasoned financial person will be able to gather information about your future plans, inform you of options, help guide you in considering what's important to you, and suggest ways of dealing with those who might see your good fortune as an opportunity to ask for money. A few hours of professional fees will be well worth it.

Here's some information about the types of consultants you might consider for help with your personal finances after you've accumulated or received assets. Many require a minimum amount of assets before taking on a client.

Certified Public Accountants—professionals with accounting degrees who've passed a series of exams and interned for two years with an accounting firm. CPAs can provide income tax advice and prepare your tax return, and some can help you create a financial plan. Some CPA firms have a separate registered investment advisor subsidiary where they can provide investment capability, but most will refer you to a type of financial advisor best suited to you. CPAs charge by the hour.

Certified Financial Planners—CFPs® must have a baccalaureate degree and pass tests administered by the College of Financial Planning. CFPs apprentice for two or three years before being awarded the official designation. Financial planners work with clients to develop a formal financial plan and help implement the plan by providing investment capability, which requires passing a series of tests administered by the Securities and Exchange Commission. CFPs may charge by the hour (fee-only planners), receive commissions on investment purchases, charge a small annual percentage of the assets under management, or a combination of these methods.

Financial Advisors—professionals who have the credentials (regulated by the Securities and Exchange Commission) to buy and sell investment instruments for their clients. In addition to stocks and bonds and similar types of investment vehicles, they may be licensed to sell certain types of insurances, as are some Certified Financial Planners. They earn commissions on purchases and/or charge a small annual percentage of the assets under management.

To learn more about choosing an advisor and for more information on investing and choosing a professional, check out the Financial Industry Regulatory Authority website: www.finra.org.

OTHER RESOURCES

This chapter addresses the first steps in investing—the basics after you start your career. As time goes on, you'll have more resources and will want to invest in a more sophisticated way. If you have a keen interest in personal finance, or even if you don't, educating yourself about various investment options and money management is a good idea. Listed below are some periodicals, newspapers, books, and online sources that provide useful information.

- *Money Magazine*
- *Wall Street Journal*
- *Financial Times*
- *Investing for Dummies* (and others in the "Dummies" series)
- *The Motley Fool Guide for Investing for Beginners*
- www.khanacademy.org. Note: All Khan Academy content is available for free. It has excellent short videos describing 401(k), IRAs, and Roth IRAs.

The financial world is always changing, so check your bookstore for new information, Google the most up-to-date resources, and look for new apps to aid your money management.

KEY TAKEAWAYS

Here, in order of how to proceed, are investment basics:

1. Open a checking account to pay expenses and deposit income.
2. Open and fund a savings account for your emergency fund.
3. Set up a retirement plan and contribute regularly.
4. Open a second savings account to accumulate money for future desires and needs, like a house, a baby, a trip to Paris, grad school, an investment portfolio.
5. When you change jobs, transfer your retirement funds to your new company or to an IRA account you've established with a financial institution.
6. Educate yourself about investing.
7. Hire a financial professional if and when you need one.

Before, During, and After College

14

Your Personal Money Philosophy

As you work your way through *Financial Basics,* be aware of those money-management techniques that appeal to you. They will help you begin to develop your personal philosophy of money—fundamental principles that you can rely on to guide you through your financial life.

In this chapter we'll explore some examples of some financial ways of thinking—ideas you may want to adopt as your own.

GIVING THANKS

Kyle used to dread bill paying. She hated watching her checking account balance decline. One morning while having coffee with her friend, Jane described a way of giving thanks that was meaningful to her. Kyle listened, was intrigued, and that evening wrote a list of all the things in life she was grateful for. She discovered listing her blessings rather than dwelling on misfortune, highlighting positive aspects of life rather than perceived failures, elevated her mood and gave her a sense of peace. She initiated the practice of giving thanks each day for the good things in her life.

This daily exercise found its way into her financial life. As she fearfully approached her desk to pay her bills, she remembered the lesson of gratitude and decided to apply the concept to bill paying.

With each payment she makes, Kyle thinks of the benefits received: electricity/light, gas/warmth, and car payment/reliable transportation. She gives thanks for these things and sends each payment with gratitude that she has the resources to pay. She doesn't begrudge her creditors and lament her declining bank balance. Instead of holding tight to her money, she gladly pays her bills. This doesn't mean that she is a spendthrift. Far from it. She practices good financial management, and she trusts that abundance will circulate back to her.

Kyle no longer hates to pay her bills, and she is convinced her new attitude of thankfulness creates a positive energy around her money. She believes that she is more prosperous today and that it's due to her new attitude toward money.

SHARING

Students are interested in volunteer activities and commit time to worthy projects. A recent news article featured a group of students who spent their spring break building houses for Habitat for Humanity—a splendid gesture of giving something of yourself to another.

A vice president for finance at a small private college counsels graduating students to "give five." She suggests that after getting a full-time job, the graduate give 5% of his or her monthly take-home pay to charitable and arts organizations that are doing work the person believes is important.

She goes on to advise new graduates to give five hours a month as a volunteer to an organization where they can make a difference. She believes giving five will enhance the graduates' lives as well as the community around them.

Marie loves to tell how she began to share. Her mother had instilled the concept of philanthropy when she was a child, telling Marie that she would see a benefit if she shared part of her money. When Marie started her new career, she gave money to charitable organizations and sat back waiting for money to flow back to her. Nothing happened.

Chagrined, she challenged her mother on the philosophy of sharing. Her mother smiled and told her the most important part of sharing was to do it freely, without thoughts of rewards. Marie, trusting her mother, donated money again. This time she chose organizations she believed were doing important work. She contributed to a shelter for women and a local ballet company.

As she wrote her monthly checks, she wished the organizations well. She imagined a new blanket for a woman in the shelter and the next performance of Swan Lake, a tradition she and her mother, once a ballerina, shared. After three years of sending donations, she began to volunteer with the ballet company working on set designs and then agreed to serve on their board. During her first board meeting, she met the love of her life.

Marie says it's all about cause and effect. If you open up a door, one thing leads to the next. And, in the end, she believes she gained more from her contributions than the organizations that received her time and money.

MONEY AND EMOTIONS

Money issues are emotionally charged for many people. It's easy to let worry and fear pervade consciousness and assume a prominent place in life. Some people deal with these emotions by being contemptuous about money matters. *Money* is a dirty word to them, and they're proud they don't waste time balancing their bank account or adhering to a spending plan. Deep down, though, they invest a lot of energy worrying about money. They haven't solved their money issues, only buried them.

Others are frightened of money. Sometimes they can't even articulate the fear. They only know money makes them nervous and they would rather not think about their finances. But, of course, they do think about it. Their fear doesn't leave.

Some people believe it is too hard to keep track of money. They think they lack the ability to manage their finances and do the minimum amount to get by.

The only answer to these money fears and worries is to take control. Instead of letting money have power over you, dispel money emotions and anxiety by taking responsibility. Taking responsibility means paying bills on time, spending below one's means, and saving part of one's income. This need not take a huge amount of your time. Use the suggestions throughout *Financial Basics*. Establish a weekly routine to deal with finances—set aside an hour during a quiet time of the week, maybe Sunday afternoon. Find your own best way to manage your money—a way that allows you to be mellow with money.

When working with clients who had difficulty managing their money, I was always pleased to see that those people who clearly wanted to become better money handlers did so. I invariably found when clients were sincere about improving, they quickly learned how to take charge. Understanding basics about finances gave them the confidence to improve.

With knowledge, you *can* overcome your fears. With practice, over time, you *can* become a mellow and a better money manager.

FEELING PROSPEROUS

Jarrett realized he was investing a lot of emotional energy in money. He worried about money, wanted more money, and dreamed about the things he could buy if he had enough money. Money consumed his mind. He thought he would never have enough to live in the manner he desired. Over time he came to understand that if he were responsible with his money, not parsimonious, but spent within his means, if he stopped worrying whether he had enough but trusted there would be resources available, he'd have plenty.

Now, Jarrett believes if he feels prosperous, he will be prosperous. He says if he allows breathing space in his life around money—and that means having a little extra put aside and not worrying if he has enough—he has more than enough.

Jarrett still loves and acquires beautiful things, but now he does it in a relaxed, fun way. He spends money within his resources, he saves money, and he does not invest emotional energy in worrying about money.

While exploring Jarrett's philosophy, the word *nest egg* comes to mind. You can also think of it as your emergency fund. If you have a nest egg or emergency fund, you will feel more protected. Clients tell me if they have money put aside that's not earmarked, that's just there for security, they, paradoxically, seem to spend less. The compulsion to spend is gone. They feel more centered around money. But if they don't have a safety net, they feel nervous and fiscally stretched. At these times of money tension, they tend to buy, usually on credit, to buoy themselves with possessions. The feelings of need and associated compulsive spending disappear when they feel prosperous by having a reserve of money. They don't deny themselves, they enjoy possessions that are important to them, but they don't give themselves what they don't need just to satisfy wild, out-of-control feelings that pop up when they're feeling financially lacking.

While you're still in school, establish your nest egg or emergency fund. It needn't be large—maybe $50 to $250 to start. Set up a special savings account at your bank and add to your reserve as time goes on. Enjoy your special cache of funds. Notice your feelings around money. When you pay your bills, reflect on your finances over the last few weeks. Has your spending behavior changed in any way? Try feeling prosperous for six months and watch how it affects the rest of your life.

When you develop a personal philosophy of money, you begin to understand yourself and you take charge. You can give thanks for what you have, or share your money with the community, or become mellow with money by examining your fears, or you can practice feeling prosperous, thereby becoming prosperous. Remember, it's about developing a unique philosophy of money that enables you to incorporate basic money-management principles in your everyday life. Whatever you choose to adopt for yourself, think of it as a positive affirmation toward your desired goals.

15

Your Story

You have read students' stories and reflected on the money-management lessons they learned when they went to college. Now it's time to write your own story. Your story will give you the opportunity to identify your strong financial practices and name those areas you want to improve.

Our attitudes about money start early and are usually learned from those closest to us. Begin by examining the attitudes about money by those who raised you.

MY MOTHER OR FEMALE INFLUENCE

Complete the following sentences. Write as much as you need to fully explain.

- **My mother's attitude toward money is**

_____

_____

_____

_____

_____

- My mother manages money by

_____
_____
_____
_____

- Concerning money, my mother always told me

_____
_____
_____
_____

MY FATHER OR MALE INFLUENCE

Complete the following sentences. Write as much as you need to fully explain.

- My father's attitude toward money is

_____
_____
_____
_____

- My father manages money by

_____
_____
_____
_____

- Concerning money, my father always told me

_____
_____
_____
_____

You may be surprised at what you discover about your family's financial practices. It could be a positive recognition of good money handling, or you might realize that one or more of the adults in your life are still learning how to manage their finances. Now is the time to decide if you will emulate these influences or find a better way to manage your money.

Our peers and siblings provide additional influence in our lives, and their attitudes about money will help you discover your own beliefs. Complete the following sentences to further delve into your influences.

- **My best friend handles his/her money by**

_____

_____

_____

_____

_____

_____

- **My sibling handles money by**

_____

_____

_____

_____

_____

_____

- **I disapprove of the way _____ handles his/her money because**

_____

_____

_____

_____

_____

_____

Carefully review your responses to these statements, especially the last one. Sometimes we reflect our own behavior when viewing others critically. If you don't approve of someone's money handling, there may be some components of that disapproval that are present in your actions. Think carefully about how you react to your negative feelings about others' financial behavior. Do you react negatively to another's financial activities because it mirrors your own?

Handling money effectively is a skill that requires thoughtfulness, awareness, knowledge, and experience. Is there someone you know who serves as a role model? A parent, a friend, a neighbor, a teacher, an employer, a well-known businessperson, or perhaps a media or published spokesperson? Someone you believe possesses mastery over his or her finances? Take this time to write a sentence about your role model's successful money-management techniques.

- **I think _____ successfully manages his/her finances because**

_____

_____

_____

_____

_____

_____

Now answer the following questions about your own money-management process. Use these questions and answers as catalysts to examine your attitudes.

- **I had an allowance as a child, and I usually spent it this way:**

_____

_____

_____

_____

_____

_____

- **I _____ saved part of my allowance, earnings, and cash gifts.**
  - ☐ always
  - ☐ never
  - ☐ sometimes

- **I control my spending by**
  - ☐ paying cash.
  - ☐ returning my purchases.
  - ☐ putting merchandise on hold to think it over.
  - ☐ spending what I want.

- **I _____ pay my bills on time.**
  - ☐ always
  - ☐ usually
  - ☐ rarely

- **I have a savings account.**
  - ☐ yes
  - ☐ no

- **I balance my checkbook every month.**
  - ☐ yes
  - ☐ no

- **I have _____ credit card(s).**

- **I pay _____ on my credit card each month.**
  - ☐ the balance due
  - ☐ the minimum payment
  - ☐ whatever I can afford

- **I don't have to worry about money—someone will bail me out if I get into trouble.**
  - ☐ yes
  - ☐ no
  - ☐ maybe

- **I don't worry about money—I will pay my debts when I graduate from college and start earning a salary.**
  - ☐ yes
  - ☐ no

- I want to start my professional life with as little debt as possible, so I am careful not to spend more than necessary.
    - ☐ yes
    - ☐ no

- When it comes to money, I am afraid that

_____

_____

_____

_____

Using the information generated from the above exercises, make a list of your money strengths and weaknesses. Write these qualities quickly. Keep the pen moving. Don't edit yourself; you are looking for as long a list as possible. Write down everything you can think of.

STRENGTHS	WEAKNESSES
_____	_____
_____	_____
_____	_____
_____	_____
_____	_____
_____	_____
_____	_____
_____	_____

Take each strength on your list, write it again, and compliment yourself.

Strength: I pay my bills on time.
Compliment: I am a responsible money manager.

Strength: I pay my credit card balance in full each month, and if I ever find myself unable to do so, I reduce my discretionary expenditures so that I can quickly pay off the bill.
Compliment: I am realistic and the master of my finances.

- **Strength:**

_____

_____

_____

- **Compliment:**

_____

_____

_____

- **Strength:**

_____

_____

_____

- **Compliment:**

_____

_____

_____

- **Strength:**

_____

_____

_____

- **Compliment:**

_____

_____

_____

Keep the list of strengths in a place where you will see it often. Rejoice in your strengths. Relish your ability to compliment yourself.

Do the same exercise with your weaknesses: write the weakness, why you think you do it, and the consequence. Know that in time you can move your weaknesses to the strength page.

Weakness: I am borrowing as much money in student loans as I can get.

Why I do it: I want to enjoy life while I am young.

Consequence: I don't know if I will be able to repay the money or not—I may be strapped for money when I graduate and begin paying off my loans.

- **Weakness:**

  _____
  _____
  _____

- **Why I do it:**

  _____
  _____
  _____

- **Consequence:**

  _____
  _____
  _____

- **Weakness:**

  _____
  _____
  _____

- **Why I do it:**

  _____
  _____

- **Consequence:**

  _____
  _____
  _____

- **Weakness:**

  _____

  _____

  _____

- **Why I do it:**

  _____

  _____

  _____

- **Consequence:**

  _____

  _____

  _____

The path to restructuring your weaknesses into strengths is shaped by taking small steps. It would be nice to resolve all your money problems in one fell swoop, but that's not realistic. Look over your list of weaknesses. Pick one you fear most, the one that makes your skin prickle when you read it. What is one small thing you could do to deal with this problem? Know that you don't have to solve the problem now. Find one small thing you can do to begin to change this weakness into a strength.

- **My biggest money weakness:**

  _____

  _____

  _____

  _____

  _____

- **One small effort to begin to change:**

  _____

  _____

  _____

  _____

  _____

  _____

Let's suppose you're borrowing as much as you can in student loans. Your first step is to go to www.nslds.ed.gov and find out what you've borrowed in federal student loans. Print out your page. Take some time to read through the report. Pat yourself on the back for gaining knowledge about your finances.

When you feel ready to address your loans again, your second step is review any private loans you may have taken out. Collect the information, review, and again feel the power this knowledge gives you.

Your third step is to create your own complete list of student loans—federal and private. Write down the interest rate you are paying and the monthly payment required once you leave school. Reflect on this total and whether the funds borrowed have been necessary for your basic education.

Finally, when it comes time to apply for funds for the new academic year, pull out your list and review. Does this information change your mind about how much you want to borrow for the coming year?

Give yourself time every month to read your strengths and review your progress on your money weaknesses. Perhaps after you pay your bills you reward yourself by reaffirming your strengths. Take a small step every month to master your finances.

LOOK TO THE FUTURE

Take some time to dream. How do you want to leave college? How do you envision your financial situation at graduation? What would be the best, most advantageous position for you to start your professional career? Is this vision achievable?

- **My financial situation at graduation will be**

_____

_____

_____

_____

_____

_____

• **Write down the steps you will take to attain your dream.**

1. _____
   _____
   _____
   _____
   _____

2. _____
   _____
   _____
   _____
   _____

3. _____
   _____
   _____
   _____
   _____

4. _____
   _____
   _____
   _____

You have written your own story. You've examined the roots of your relationship with money and reflected on your strengths and weaknesses. Stories are edited and rewritten. Stories evolve. With greater awareness and knowledge over time, your money story will change too.

Revisit this chapter at the beginning of each school year. Enjoy the progress you've made in understanding your personal finances and working toward your dreams. Recreate the exercises where you see changes are still needed.

If you can master your finances and money-handling practices while in school, you'll have a lifetime of power over money. You will be in charge—you will be a master of your finances.

16

A Note to Parents

The world is more complicated than ever, especially when it comes to finances. College students are usually eager to assume independence, and most of them are responsible, but they're inexperienced and may get into difficulty because they're too trusting or too busy or unaware. Here are some ideas for steadying the financial ship your child is sailing.

SHARING FINANCIAL FACTS OF LIFE

You may have talked with your children over the years, explaining financial matters. You may have disclosed your family's financial situation. Or, perhaps you didn't. A financial services company reported that parents find talking to their children about money more difficult than talking about sex.

Some people want to keep their financial information confidential, some have been brought up to believe that money is a subject not discussed with children, and others are embarrassed by their financial management. If you haven't disclosed the family finances to your children, I urge you to reconsider. They may have a completely erroneous idea of your financial capability and are expecting more from you than you can provide. This is also an opportunity to teach them about money management.

As a further incentive to taking a proactive approach to financial literacy with your children, *The Wall Street Journal* referenced a report from Higher One that found that only 58% of students felt prepared to manage their money. And while many freshmen have good intentions about following a budget and paying their bills on time, the survey noted that over a three-year period, the number of students planning to take these steps and other proper money-management actions has declined.

FINANCIAL AID

As your student begins applying for college, you will undoubtedly fill out a Free Application for Federal Student Aid (FAFSA) for financial aid. You will be required to report income and assets and liabilities on this form, and if you haven't talked with your student about the family finances, this is an opportunity to discuss what you can afford to contribute to the college costs and what you expect from your child.

Once your student is notified of acceptances, schools will get back to you with a financial aid package. You and your student need to figure out how to make up any shortfall.

This is the time to create or revisit the college spending plan and fill in any financial aid, work-study, grants, and scholarships as the sources of funds. This will tell you and your student how much more money you will have to provide. Sources of funds are whatever you can provide through savings, earnings, and borrowing, and your student's college savings accounts, summer jobs, part-time work, and student loans.

Keep in mind that if your financial situation changes significantly—an illness, a lost job, reduced pay—contact the university financial aid office to see if your student can qualify for more aid.

A Sallie Mae study shows that middle- and lower-income families typically underestimate college expenses. For example, when asked how much they believe they should budget for books, students replied, $655. The College Board's suggested annual book budget is $1,200—almost twice as much as the students expected.

Be sure to check the suggested budget provided by college websites and refine it according to any additional information you have.

LOANS

Make sure your student understands that student loans taken out will have to be repaid once leaving college—with or without a degree. This may seem evident, after all, this is a *loan*, but more than one student has misunderstood the repayment requirement, particularly if they left school without a degree.

I recently talked with a young woman raised on the East Coast who wanted to go to the University of Oregon, but the out-of-state tuition seemed too high for the money available. "Use student loans," Molly's parents advised. So she did—attended and graduated, loved her college experience, and was startled upon graduation to learn she had to repay the loans. She had no idea. Remember, these students are teenagers with little financial experience. What seems obvious to you may be a mystery to them.

Make sure your student knows that grants and scholarships provide funds that do not have to be repaid, but student loans, plus interest, will have to be repaid starting six to nine months after graduation or when dropping out of school.

Advise your student to keep a running total of loan obligations and the expected monthly payment after graduation. Refer to the worksheets in this book or other online resources. Counsel your student to be cautious about private loans. They are more expensive because interest is not deferred until the student graduates. Chances are you'll be required to co-sign for private loans, which don't have the protections federally backed loans have.

I've mentioned the following letter in a previous chapter, but the information is so striking, I want to be sure you read it too. In 2012, Indiana University sent a letter to all students who had student loans projecting how much debt they were on track to graduate with and what their monthly payments would be. Amazingly, one year after the first letter was sent, borrowing declined by 12.4 percent. Apparently the information helped students limit borrowing to actual needs rather than inflating loans to satisfy wants.

This is why it is so important for your student to keep a running total of money borrowed and the monthly payments.

Will you have to borrow to help fund college expenses? If so, remember, it will be for at least four years, not just the first year, and your monthly repayment begins sixty days after the last disbursement for the school year. (Only students' federal student loan repayments are deferred until leaving school.) Do you have younger children who will later need assistance from you? You'll need to plan ahead for these expenses and not overextend your borrowing. Again, share this information with your children. Make them partners in this financial exploration and decision making. Each school has a net price calculator that shows how much grant aid students receive at their school, and there is all kinds of online assistance to help you work through these matters. Here are a few examples, but make an online search to be sure you have the latest and best information:

www.collegecost.ed.gov
www.finaid.org
www.studentloans.gov
www.nslds.ed.gov

If you decide to take out loans to help your student, there are two basic types: government PLUS Loans and private loans. Be sure to compare the terms of each type. You may find a private loan is more advantageous if you have a good credit history and a certain income level.

You will have to decide on the best approach for your situation. I know it is unlikely, but know that government loans will not have to be repaid if your child dies, whereas private loans will be. I'm reminded of a news story a few years ago about a gardener who earned little money but co-signed loans for his son to attend an expensive music school. Sadly, the son was killed in an automobile accident shortly after graduation, and the gardener was responsible for over $100,000 of debt. If you take out private loans or co-sign for loans, I recommend purchasing a term life insurance policy for your child for the amount of the private loans. It will be inexpensive and financially protect you if the unthinkable happens.

If you are willing to borrow to help fund college, who is going to be responsible for repaying your loans? Do you expect your student to assume payment responsibility after graduation? Are you willing to repay the loan? Do you want to share the responsibility? Get this out on the table now so that you and your student can plan knowledgeably.

PROPRIETARY SCHOOLS

Be cautious about proprietary (for profit) schools where costs are high for programs and loans are readily available. Corinthian Colleges Inc. recently declared bankruptcy and left many students with oppressive student loan debt and no degree. Research these schools before signing up. Go online to gather more information. Are there complaints about usury practices? What is the graduation rate? What is the average student debt at graduation? What kind of salary can a graduate expect to earn? Do the earnings justify the debt?

BE REALISTIC

Your student may want to go to a school that the family cannot afford. Sometimes a student hears about a school from a teacher and decides that would be a good place to go. Or maybe a friend is going to an out-of-state public institution that charges significantly more for non-residents.

One of my client's sons wanted to go to the University of Colorado, but they lived in Ohio. The higher tuition would have been a stretch for them, and their son couldn't give them a good reason for going out of state to school. I advised the parents not to spend money they could ill afford on the higher tuition. I told them they could quote me. Their son eventually decided on The Ohio State University and had an excellent college experience.

If your student aspires to a college that is not financially feasible, take this opportunity to go through the numbers and demonstrate that adjustments to the college choice must be made. Many students go on to graduate school, and your student might plan to attend that favored college later, after receiving an undergraduate degree. Hold firm. You need to protect your own financial well being as well as that of your child.

CREDIT CARDS

Students can no longer easily get credit cards without a parent's signature or proof that they have the resources to make payments. Be careful about signing for a credit card if you expect your child to make the monthly payments. If they do not make timely payments, it will negatively affect your credit rating.

However, credit cards are useful. They're more secure than debit or bank cards, disputed charges get more attention, and if the card is stolen or used illegally, the holder's liability is usually capped at $50.

I believe it's prudent to help your student understand how to use a credit card responsibly and get some experience with one before entering the workforce. It's also a way to begin to establish a credit history, which will be important after graduation when purchasing a car and renting an apartment. Even prospective employers check credit histories to gain more information about the job applicant's record of responsibility.

Unfortunately, some people go a little crazy with the possibilities of charging and have to learn how to control their spending. This is a good time for a young person to learn credit card management in a controlled way. Look into getting your student a secured credit card in their name. A deposit is given to the credit card company in advance, let's say $500. The student can charge up to that amount, just as a regular credit card has a limit. You make your student responsible for paying the credit card bill every month, emphasizing that on-time payments will affect his or her credit history and that 35% of a person's credit score is based on making timely payments. A secured credit card provides the learning experience for your student to handle a credit card while limiting your liability to the $500 you've already deposited as a guarantee. Since one of the reasons for getting a credit card is to establish a credit history, be sure to confirm with the credit card institution that the payment history will be reported to a credit bureau.

As I've mentioned in previous chapters, if your student can't control spending, suggest cutting up the card and using cash or a debit card until he or she is more confident managing a credit card.

SCHOLARSHIPS

Financial aid people tell me it is important to apply for scholarships, lots of them, and to do it *every* year. Some scholarships are given for need, others for good grades, some for unique talents or interests. The application process is a pain, and your student may complain, but the rewards could be significant and reduce the need for loans.

CHECK IN

Sometimes students get into financial difficulties without their parents' knowledge. They may not be paying their bills on time, thereby injuring their credit rating; they may have borrowed more money than you thought they would; they may be paying for things they no longer need or use.

Financial aid directors tell me that one problem that's been increasing is students borrowing university emergency or bridge loan funds. These loans are typically under $2,000, and the student has to apply for the money, make a case for the need, and repay the loan the following school term. Some students borrow but can't afford to repay, so they continue to renew the loan each term. They're treating the bridge loan like a credit card.

One mother told me about her son who signed up for a Gold's Gym membership for the summer between his freshman and sophomore years but forgot to cancel his contract when he went back to school. The monthly fee was charged against his credit card, but he never reviewed the charges on his monthly credit card statement, just paid the bill every month and unknowingly continued paying monthly dues for two years until a letter from Gold's

Gym arrived at his parents' home requesting an updated credit card expiration date. You can imagine how that conversation went.

Financial Summit

Have a periodic fiscal check-in—call it a financial summit. Let your student know before leaving for college that this will be a regular thing and you expect to review the financial situation on the first visit home.

Initiate the fiscal summit by asking if there have been any financial surprises. Together, review bank and credit card statements. Be aware of deadlines for important bills like tuition and dorm fees. Are those bills being paid on time? Are there bank charges for overdrafts? Is spending in line with the original plan? Are there payments to organizations that were unexpected, like club dues or lab fees or cellular data plans? Does the spending plan need to be adjusted? Discuss how expenditures are being tracked and if the checking account is regularly reviewed. Is there a written running total of student loans and the expected monthly payment?

Make the fiscal summit fun, a learning opportunity for your student. End the fiscal summit with dinner out to celebrate the progress. Make it a positive experience.

FEDERAL INCOME TAXES

For lower- and moderate-income parents, be sure to check out any tax deductions available to you if you claim your student as an exemption.

If you have taken out PLUS loans or private loans for college expenses, you may be able to deduct the interest paid each year either as an itemized deduction or in addition to the standard deduction.

Check current tax rules for the most up-to-date information.

YOUR GOAL

The end goal is your child receiving a degree from a four-year institution. That means financial planning for the four or five years it'll take to achieve that goal. It will be worth the effort—students with a college degree earn far more than high school graduates or students with associate degrees. And that's why careful planning is important. One big reason for students dropping out of school is they've not taken into account the full costs, not just for one year, but for the entire college program.

Six to nine months after leaving school with or without a degree, those student loans' monthly repayment begins. If the student drops out of school, they forgo the higher salary a four-year college degree would have engendered.

The *New York Times* reported on a woman who had gone to college after high school working toward a degree in education. She'd had to drop out before finishing because of her limited finances. She left school with $33,000 in student loans. She took menial jobs, often working more than one job just to get by. She was not able to pay all her bills, and her student loan debt grew to $95,000. She declared bankruptcy, but student loans are not wiped out with bankruptcy. Only her medical bills were forgiven. She persisted through the courts, and at age sixty-eight, living on social security, a judge finally eliminated her debt. This is a cautionary tale for planning carefully for the entire college career and earning a degree.

BE THERE

So get involved. If you need to review financial principles, consider reading this book concurrently with your student. Choose a relevant chapter, read, discuss, and do exercises suggested in the chapter. Help your child become a master of money.

17

A Postscript to Grandparents

Grandparents have wisdom and life experiences to pass on to grandchildren. Some have certain talents or interests that may be relevant; some have financial resources that can smooth the way for college-bound grandchildren. The following are ways you can help your young people as they prepare for college.

The financial aspects of going to college have changed dramatically. The cost of college has risen a lot faster than most other costs in the past twenty years. For example, in 2015, a suggested annual book budget is $1,200. Tuition and room and board at a private school averages $34,193 a year, and public universities are averaging $16,482.

While you may have provided much of the money needed when your children went to college, financial-aid administrators report that parents are no longer as willing or able to support their children to the extent that previous generations did.

Divorced parents especially seem to have difficulty managing financial decisions about college. One administrator expressed concern that children become pawns in the college support discussions, and their best interests are not kept in focus by the parents.

Because so many of our children are having their families later in life, they may be caught in a financial vise when it comes time to pay for college. If they haven't saved adequately for retirement, they may be trying to pay for college and simultaneously catching up on funding their retirement accounts. This is a new pattern, and the old financial-planning models may not work for them. If I advise a client on making a decision between whether to pay for college or fund retirement, I reluctantly put retirement first.

Students are pressed to look for other sources of college funding. Grant money used to be more plentiful, but federal need-based grants have not kept pace with inflation and tuition increases. In the Seventies a needy student could count on the Pell grant covering 75% of the cost at a public institution. Today, that figure is 30%. Rather than increasing grant support, Congress raised the limits on the amount of federally backed loans so that students could borrow more money from lenders to make up the difference.

Scholarships are still available, and while students are encouraged to look for opportunities, scholarships rarely provide all the funds needed. That leaves summer jobs and part-time work during the school year, which no longer adequately cover college costs.

The last resort is student loans. The amount owed at graduation continues to climb. According to the latest *U.S. News and World Report,* 69% of graduates have loans, and the average debt at graduation is $28,400. Even though a college degree is a good investment, it's hard to watch this generation taking on high debt so early in life.

It probably never occurred to your parents to offer financial help for your children's education. But there's been such a dramatic change in the financing of higher education that grandparents may want to reconsider their role.

You may be better off at this stage of life than your grandparents were when you enrolled in college. You may have recently inherited money that you know you won't need in retirement. Perhaps you've already retired but you aren't as active as you hoped and have decided to work part-time—not for the money, but for the joy of being productive. Possibly you've paid off your mortgage and have extra cash.

If you're in your retirement years, it's a good time to review your finances and estate plan. If you see that you have more than enough, helping those deserving grandchildren is an option for you. For example, you could give them the money they need to finish financing their education and deduct it from the legacy that would eventually go to them or their parents.

Consider giving your grandchild money in the form of a loan, either interest bearing or not, to be paid back over a certain number of years. Draw up papers to formalize the agreement so there are no questions later on. You can always forgive the loan at some point if the circumstances seem right to you.

Shifting some assets to grandchildren as they go to college will reduce the financial strain on their parents and give you the pleasure of helping out. It's a tradition that can be passed on in the family.

You can give a person up to $14,000 a year without gift tax consequences. If you're married, your spouse can also give up to $14,000 annually to each individual. You can give them appreciated stock or mutual funds with the same limitations. Currently you can pay your grandchild's tuition and room and board directly to the higher educational institution without gift tax restrictions. You should confirm this information before going ahead since tax laws do change from time to time.

Sometimes grandparents or an aunt or uncle want to help out with college costs but do not want the student or parents to know that they are providing funds. Some colleges will accept the money directly from a relative and report it as scholarship money to the student. The student never knows the source of the funds. If you are interested in this approach, contact the director of financial aid at your grandchild's college of choice and ask if the school can accommodate your desire to provide funds. Assure the institution that you are not expecting a tax deduction for this—it's not legal—you only want to quietly help this student. Note that the student will have to report this source of funds on the next Free Application for Federal Student Aid (FAFSA), which could impact funding levels for other forms of financial aid. You could discuss this with the financial aid director.

A gift is best given with joy and love. It doesn't entitle the benefactor to assume power over another person. But it does makes sense to talk with a grandchild you are helping financially, even setting up annual meetings at which you review the student's financial situation and progress toward a degree, and provide the benefit of your financial experience. Financial help doesn't sanction dictating career choice or forcing a certain program of study. But your help—both financial and in life experience—will give you, the grandparent, a great deal of satisfaction and will make a difference in a grandchild's life.

On the other hand, you may not have extra funds, and much as you want to see your grandchildren succeed, you can't provide financial support. What if your grandson comes to you and says, "Grandma, I won't be able to finish my degree without another loan, and I need a co-signer to qualify. Would you please sign for the loan?" I think it would be hard to say no, but I urge you to be careful. Would you be able to afford monthly payments on a loan if he couldn't make the payments? How would taking on this expense affect your lifestyle? I've read newspaper reports about grandparents whose monthly social security payments have been reduced to pay off a co-signed delinquent student loan.

You may think your grandson would never put you at risk, and that's probably true, but we can't predict the future. Just a few years ago college students were not able to get good jobs after graduation. They were returning home to live with their parents because they couldn't afford to pay rent. While the employment situation is improving, you've lived long enough to know there are economic cycles and that a prudent person plans for downturns. If you cannot risk your assets, tell your grandson that much as you'd like to help him, you simply can't co-sign for the loan because, while you know your he's responsible and fully intending to repay the loan, sometimes life doesn't go as we planned and you'd have no way of coming up with the extra money to make the loan payments. You don't have a steady income from a job. You're living on savings and social security and *your* goal is not to be dependent upon your children in your old age.

Maybe you can offer support in other ways. If you are financially astute, offer to review your grandson's projected college expenses, looking for ways to cut costs. You could ask him how much he's already borrowed in student loans and what the monthly payment will be once after graduation. If he doesn't know, help him develop a spreadsheet with the information. What kind of salary will he be earning in his chosen career? Will he make enough after taxes and other withholdings to pay his living expenses and student loans? Do you have connections to the business community that might garner a better-paying summer job? Offer to do a scholarship search online to find additional sources of funds. You could work together to craft submissions for scholarships. Sometimes teamwork makes the process easier.

Being there for our families doesn't always involve money, and our resources may be richer in experience and knowledge—a different kind of wealth to be passed down.

Glossary of
Financial Terms

401(k) plan—A retirement plan funded with the employee's pre-tax dollars. The employer may have an option to match the employee's contribution.

403(b) plan—A tax-sheltered retirement plan for people who work in tax-exempt organizations.

Annual fee—A fee assessed each year by credit card companies. You do not have to write a check for this fee; it is automatically added to your credit card debt. The annual fee is sometimes waived for the first year.

Annual percentage rate (APR)—The interest rate you pay expressed as a simple annual percentage. Every lender, including credit card companies, is required to tell you the APR. Always check the APR so you know the interest rate you are paying.

Automated teller machine (ATM)—A machine that lets you make cash withdrawals, deposits, or transfers between your accounts. If you make withdrawals from an ATM not affiliated with your financial institution, you may be charged a transaction fee.

Bank balance—The amount of money the bank shows in an account at a given time. This is not the true balance of your account since there may be checks or deposits that have not yet been processed by the bank.

Bank statement—A list of all the transactions and current balance on a specific account. Usually mailed monthly and often available online.

Cancelled check—A check that has been paid and cleared the bank. Can be used as proof of payment and should be kept for a year, if your bank returns cancelled checks with your monthly statement.

Cashier's check—A special type of check issued at your request by a financial institution made payable to a specified receiver. You give the financial institution the money to cover the amount of check, plus a handling fee. A cashier's check guarantees the receiver that funds are available to cover the check.

Certificate of deposit (CD)—A savings device for money deposited in the bank for a fixed amount of time in exchange for a higher interest rate. CDs can be purchased for as little as three months. If you take the money out before the term of the CD, you usually pay a penalty.

Check card—A plastic card that looks like a credit card and works like a check. Be sure to note the amount of the purchase in your check register because the amount is automatically deducted from your checking account. Sometimes called a debit card.

Check register—A journal used to record the checks you write, deposits, fees, ATM withdrawals, and check or debit card transactions. This is where you keep track of all your checking account transactions and your current balance in the account.

Clear—A check has cleared when it has been deducted from your account by your bank.

Collateral—Anything of value pledged to a lender until a loan is repaid; e.g., a car is the collateral on an auto loan. Collateral can be seized by the lender if the loan is not paid.

Compound interest—Interest earned on principal plus the accumulated interest that was earned earlier. Interest may be calculated daily, monthly, quarterly, or annually. This is why credit card debt is so expensive. You are paying interest on the amount charged plus accumulated interest on the account.

Co-signer—Someone who signs a credit agreement along with the borrower. The co-signer is legally obligated to assume responsibility for loan repayment if the borrower doesn't.

Credit bureau—An organization that maintains records on credit and personal financial history. Information is available for a fee to creditors to assess your ability to pay. Can also be accessed by potential employers.

Credit limit—The maximum amount of money you can spend in a credit agreement. Credit cards usually carry a credit limit.

Credit rating—An evaluation of the borrower's credit worthiness based on the borrower's ability and willingness to pay back loans. Typically devised by a credit bureau or financial institution. *See* FICO.

Creditor—An organization or individual that lends money or to whom money is owed.

Debit card—*See* **check card.**

Debt—Amount(s) you owe and are obligated to pay back, like student loans, credit card charges, and installment loans.

Default—Failure to repay a financial obligation according to the terms of the agreement, or failure to submit requests for deferment or cancellation on time. Defaults are registered with credit bureaus, may result in legal action, and may limit future borrowing possibilities.

Deferment—An approved postponement of loan payments for a specific period of time.

Dividends—Money paid to a stock shareholder out of a company's earnings.

Endorse—To sign your name on the back of a check that's made out to you. Once you sign the check it is like cash; you can get cash, deposit the money into your account, or sign the check over to someone else. It is best not to endorse a check until you are ready to use it; if you lose the endorsed check, someone could cash it, and you have no recourse.

Federal direct student loan program (FDSLP, FDSL, FDLP, FDL)—Federal loan programs where the student borrows directly from the government.

Federal Educational Loan Program (FELP), Federal Family Education Loan Program (FFELP)—Federal loan programs where the student borrows from a commercial lender, but the loans are guaranteed against default by the federal government.

FICO—An acronym for Fair Isaac Corporation, a company that devised the widely used credit risk score model.

Financial aid—The combination of grants, scholarships, work-study, and student loans provided by state and federal governments, the school, and private sponsors.

Fixed rate—A rate of interest that does not change over the life of the loan. Other loans may carry a variable interest rate. Always confirm the rate and type of interest when you take out a loan.

Free Application for Federal Student Aid (FAFSA)—Form for applying for federal student aid.

Grants—Monies awarded a student. Does not need to be repaid.

Gross income—The total amount of money from a job before deductions such as federal, state, city, and social security taxes are taken. *See also* **net income.**

Individual retirement account (IRA)—Tax-deferred plan where qualified individuals can set up a retirement account. Contributions and earnings are not taxed until withdrawn at retirement. Penalties are assessed for early withdrawal. *See also* **Roth IRA.**

Installment loan—A loan for a set amount of money that is to be repaid, usually monthly, over a period of time. An automobile loan is an example.

Interest—A fee paid for the use of money. You earn interest by depositing money into an interest-bearing account. You pay interest when you borrow money.

Lease—A contract to rent property.

Loan—Money that is borrowed with a formal promise to repay over time with interest.

Money market funds—Short-term investments that are similar to savings accounts. Usually pay a higher interest rate.

Mutual funds—Investment of funds made up of cash and securities and directed by a manager who buys and sells on behalf of investors. Think of it as a big pot where a number of investors pool their money to buy investments.

Net income—Often called take-home pay, this is the amount of money you receive from your job after taxes and other deductions are taken from the gross amount.

Non-sufficient funds (NSF)—Not enough money in a checking account to cover a check. This is the official name for a "bounced" check. The check will be returned to the person or business trying to cash the check, they will probably be charged a fee, and you will be charged a fee. You will have to make the check good by depositing sufficient funds into your account and having the check redeposited.

Overdraft protection—A line of credit on your checking account that deposits money into your account if you write a check for more than is in the account. Interest, usually at high credit card rates, is charged when this is used. Always have overdraft protection on your checking account.

Payroll deductions—Amounts subtracted from your gross pay (federal, state, and city income taxes; health, life, and disability insurance; retirement programs, etc), which results in your net income or take-home pay.

Pell grant—A federal grant for undergraduates based on need.

Perkins loan—A federal low-interest loan based on need for undergraduate and graduate students.

Personal identification number (PIN)—A code you devise to access your accounts. Protect this code information from others.

PLUS loan—A federal loan program for parents. Repayment usually starts after ninety days.

Prime rate—The interest rate that a financial institution charges its best customers.

Principal—The initial amount of a loan before interest is charged. Also, the initial amount of money deposited in an account before interest or dividends are earned.

Reconciliation—To bring into agreement the amount in your bank statement or your check register. This is balancing your bank account.

Renter's insurance—Insurance to protect personal property in rental housing such as a dormitory or an apartment.

Roth IRA—The initial contribution is made with after-tax dollars, but the earnings are allowed to accumulate without taxes.

Scholarship—Financial aid that does not have to be paid back. Sometimes awarded on need but mostly on personal achievement.

Simple interest—Interest charged or interest earned on the principal amount only. It is calculated as *principal* × *interest* × *time.*

Stafford loan—A government student loan. May be subsidized or unsubsidized; i.e., the interest is deferred or starts accruing immediately.

Supplemental Education Opportunity Grant—Federal grant awarded to undergraduate students who have exceptional financial need.

Variable rate—An interest rate that can change over time.

W-2 statement—A form that is issued by your employer showing how much you earned in a given calendar year and the payroll tax deductions. Copies of your W-2 form are sent in January to you and federal, state, and city governments.

W-4 form—A form you fill out for your employer that indicates how many deductions you wish to take. It affects the amount of federal income taxes to be withheld from your paycheck. You should change your W-4 anytime your marital status or dependents change. If you work part-time or only in the summer while a student, you may qualify for an exemption from withholding taxes. Check with your employer.

Work study programs—A federal, need-based program where undergraduate and graduate students can earn a portion of their college expenses through part-time work during the school year.

Helpful Apps and Websites

This appendix describes some helpful mobile device and computer apps and websites for assistance in managing your finances. Read the reviews to help make decisions on which apps will best meet your financial needs.

Caution: Always protect your financial data apps and websites with password or fingerprint access. While some apps make it convenient to keep you logged in, don't do so unless you have a strong password requirement to open your mobile device or computer.

HELPFUL APPS

Acorns
Bankrate
Check
Credit
CreditKarma
Dollarbird
FinMason
Goodbudget
KhanAcademy
LearnVest

Mint
MoneyWiz

Check your bank's apps that help track your money. Most are upgrading and adding new features regularly.

KEY WORDS FOR APP SEARCHES

New apps appear often, so do a key word search to learn what's available.

Banking
Budgets
Budget Tool
Checkbook
Credit Card
Digital Wallet
Financial Budgeting
Financial Calculator
Financial Planner
Finance Tracker
Investing
Money
Money Management
Money Tracker
Saving Money
Shared Payments
Spending Tracker
Student Loans

HELPFUL WEBSITES

Bankrate financial calculators, www.bankrate.com

Bureau of Labor Statistics, Occupational Outlook Handbook, www.bls.gov/ooh

Consumer Credit Counseling Service, www.credit.org/cccs

Credit Report, www.AnnualCreditReport.com

Credit Score, www.creditkarma.com

Department of Education (repayment of student loans, income-driven), www.studentaid.ed.gov/sa/ repay-loans/understand/plans/income-driven

Federal Deposit Insurance Corporation, www.fdic.gov/ deposit

Federal Student Aid, www.studentaid.ed.gov

Federal Student Loans, www.studentloans.gov

FinAid Guide to Financial Aid, www.finaid.org/calculator

Financial Calculators, http://www.financialcalculator.org

Financial Industry Regulatory Authority, www.finra.org

How to Balance a Checkbook, http://www.calculatorsoup. com/calculators/financial/checkbook-balance-calculator. php#howto

How to Write a Check, http://banking.about.com/video/ How-to-Write-a-Check.htm

Investing Information, www.investinganswers.com

Keeping Track of Spending, www.mint.com

Khan Academy (short videos on student aid, finances), www.khanacademy.org *(Note: All Khan Academy content is available for free.)*

National Center for Educational Statistics, www.nces. ed.gov/collegenavigator

National Student Loan Data System, www.nslds.ed.gov

Scholarship searches, www.fastweb.com

Student Loan Borrower Assistance, www. studentloanborrowerassistance.org

Student Loan Inventory Worksheets, www.financialbasics. org

U.S. Department of Education College Affordability & Transparency Center, www.collegecost.ed.gov

Worksheets from *Financial Basics*, www.financialbasics.org

Three organizations track and report credit information and calculate credit scores:

Equifax, www.equifax.com
Experian, www.experian.com
TransUnion, www.transunion.com

Index

Note: Page numbers in *italics* refer to worksheets.

Made in the USA
Monee, IL
23 August 2020